PRACTICAL POLE BUILDING CONSTRUCTION

PRACTICAL POLE BUILDING CONSTRUCTION

Leigh W. Seddon

Williamson Publishing Company
Charlotte, Vermont 05445

Acknowledgements & Credits

The author and publisher would like to thank the following individuals, companies, and organizations for their assistance:

American Institute of Timber Construction, American Plywood Association, American Wood Preservers Institute, J. H. Baxter Co., Stephen Coyle, Fine Homebuilding Magazine, Forest Products Laboratory (USDA), Koppers Co., National Forest Products Association, New England Builder, New England Pole Co., Brent Smith, Southern Forest Products Association, Teco Products and Testing Corp., and John Wolff.

All photographs are by the author except as noted below:

John Wolff, cover (top left), pages 31 and 101; Shrowt, courtesy of Koppers Co., cover (bottom right) and page 7 (bottom); Brent Smith, page 4; John Malmquist, courtesy of Koppers Co., pages 6 (top) and 69; courtesy of *Fine Homebuilding* magazine, © The Taunton Press, Inc. 1983, page 8; courtesy of American Institute of Timber Construction, page 11; courtesy of Wheeling Pittsburg Steel Corp., page 113; courtesy of Koppers Co., page 127 (top); courtesy of Marvin Window Co., page 127 (bottom).

Illustrations by David Sylvester
Cover design: Trezzo-Braren Studio
Interior design: Ann Aspell Book Design & Production
Typography: Villanti & Sons, Printers, Inc.
Printing: Capital City Press

Williamson Publishing Co.
Box 185
Charlotte, Vermont 05445
1-800-234-8791

Manufactured in the United States of America

20

Library of Congress Cataloging in Publication Data

Seddon, Leigh, 1951–
    Practical pole building construction.

    Bibliography: p.
    Includes index.
    1. Pole houses — Design and construction.
2. Building, Wooden. 3. Wood poles. I. Title.
TH4818.W6S43   1985   694'.2   85-9248
ISBN 0-913589-16-0 (pbk.)

Contents

PART II/BUILDING PLANS

APPENDIX

Part I

WHY BUILD WITH POLES?

CHAPTER ONE

Pole building, one of the world's oldest building techniques, has endured through the ages because of its simplicity, economy, and strength. Primitive cultures throughout the world traditionally used wooden poles embedded in the earth for building frames that were then covered with wood and thatching. These structures were easy to build, made from local materials, and could withstand flooding and high winds.

These same qualities make pole building attractive for today's building needs. The techniques of pole building have not changed much from ancient times, but the materials have. Today we have pressure-treated poles, special fasteners, and other materials that make pole building even more durable and economical.

Foundation Savings

In modern residential construction, the foundation work often accounts for 15 percent of the total budget. It is not uncommon to sink $10,000 or more in the ground before the framing even starts. Pole construction offers an economical alternative that can do away with massive poured concrete walls, earth-moving equipment, and the site disruption that such activities entail.

The foundation for a pole building is also the pole that serves as a framing member. Pressure-treated poles or posts are buried in the earth 4 to 6 feet deep, giving them tremendous vertical and lateral bearing strength. Foundation excavation is thus reduced to digging a hole for each pole. This is usually done by hand or with a power auger attached to the back of a tractor.

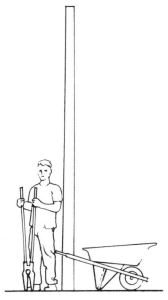

Figure 1-1. A conventional foundation requires heavy excavation equipment, cement trucks, and skilled laborers. A pole foundation requires only a posthole digger, a wheelbarrow, and some muscle power.

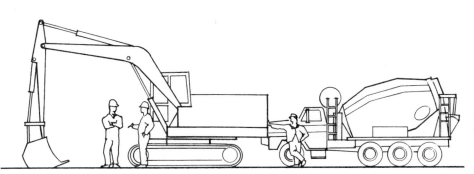

A small amount of concrete is used for a necklace around the bottom of the pole. This can be mixed by hand or poured directly from a truck if the site is accessible. A conventional (non-pole) 30 × 40 house with 4-foot deep concrete foundation walls would require approximately 20 yards of concrete for the foundation. By comparison, a pole house of the same size could be built using less than 1 yard of concrete.

A pole foundation not only saves on material costs but labor costs as well. A poured concrete foundation is a job for a professional because of the forms, equipment, and expertise needed. With pole building, there is no need to hire subcontractors for excavation and concrete work, nor to arrange your building schedule around theirs.

Structurally, a pole foundation can also be vastly superior to a poured wall, especially when you are building on poor soils. Wet clays can freeze and put 15,000 pounds of lateral pressure per square foot on the outside of a concrete wall with resultant cracking. These same forces pose no problem for a pole foundation since the pressure is evenly distributed around the pole.

Site Adaptability

Because of this unique foundation system, a pole building can be erected on a site that would prove impossible for a building with a conventional foundation. A steep hillside, for example, would require extensive terracing and earth-moving to accommodate a

The Abramson house, designed by Brent Smith, with the spring flood of the Sacramento River flowing underneath it.

A traditional pole house of African influence in North Yemen (Yemen Arab Republic).

poured foundation. This is not only expensive, but can cause serious erosion problems. Yet, on the same site, a pole foundation could be put in with little more trouble than it takes to build on level ground.

Because pole building is not limited by site contours and drainage, low-cost building sites can be used. Often a piece of land, perfectly suitable for pole building, can be bought at a bargain price because the site is considered "unbuildable."

Steep slopes, undrained soils, and periodic flooding are limitations that have traditionally forced us to build on our best land, usually prime agricultural land. Pole building can help us utilize marginal lands in an environmentally responsible way, while preserving our best agricultural soils for crop production.

Pole building also is well suited for construction at sites where it would be impossible to use standard excavation equipment. A pole cabin can be placed in a wooded area with a minimal amount of tree cutting and disruption to the forest environment. Thus the natural landscape can be preserved, minimizing soil compaction, erosion, and post-construction landscaping costs.

Modern pole buildings serve a wide variety of purposes. Shown here are a hillside house in Hawaii, a 200-cow dairy barn in Vermont, a simple lean-to barn, and a beach house in Alabama.

Framing Flexibility

Pole building also offers great flexibility in design. A pole house can be built to suit a particular site without the additional engineering and design expense that would be necessary for a conventional building. On a hillside, a pole house can easily step down the slope. In a forest, it can wind around the trees, becoming an integral part of the landscape.

Another significant advantage to pole building relates to wall framing. Because all the loads are carried by the supporting poles and girts, wall sections are non-loadbearing and need not be framed to carry the weight of the building, as in conventional construction. This opens up tremendous opportunities for using passive solar heat and natural daylight, since large sections of the walls can be glazed without worrying about structural support. Non-loadbearing walls also lower framing costs, especially those associated with superinsulated building designs.

This simplicity and flexibility in wall framing lends itself to the design of buildings with large open interior spaces, since walls are not needed to carry floors or the roof. Japanese houses take advantage of this feature and use shosi screens and other moveable dividers to partition large spaces. For barns and warehouses, pole building is ideal since the interior can be left unobstructed or partitioned off with light, economical walls.

The Moore house in North Carolina shows how a pole building can blend right into the forest environment and minimize site disruption.

Figure 1-2. Pole building is particularly suited to steep slopes. The Hillside House, which is detailed in Part 2 of the book, has a carport nestled right under the front deck.

While pole buildings are often considered unconventional in appearance (and many pole buildings are), there is no reason a pole building cannot resemble other traditional building styles. With different roofs and siding, a pole building can change from a New England colonial to a California ranch house.

Figure 1-3. This pole cabin, detailed in Part 2 of the book, shows how pole construction lends itself to passive solar heating since the walls are non-loadbearing.

Structural Stability

A properly designed pole building can withstand stresses that would flatten conventional structures. In this regard, pole houses have proven themselves through hurricanes, floods, and earthquakes during the last 25 years.

Because a pole frame is embedded in the earth, the poles transmit lateral forces on the walls (such as from wind loading) directly into the ground where they are absorbed. This makes for an extremely resilient structure even in heavy winds, tornadoes, and flooding which would rip a conventional house right off its foundation.

Another advantage of pole structures is their fire resistance. Conventional frame houses burn very quickly, the framing serving almost as kindling. While framed wall sections in a pole house also burn quickly, the pole frame itself does not. Because of their large size, poles and large beams tend to char on the surface which inhibits further burning. Thus the supporting structure of a pole house can withstand fires that would collapse a building with conventional wood framing or even steel framing which cannot withstand high temperatures.

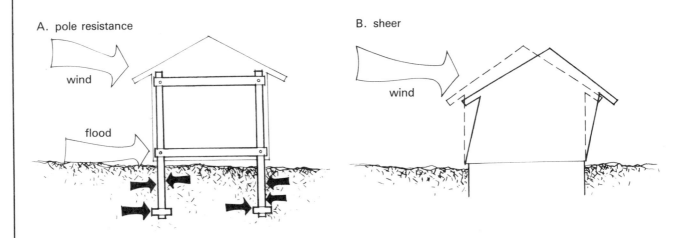

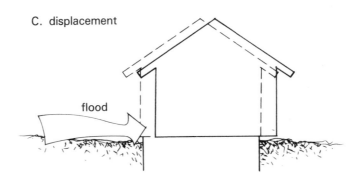

Figure 1-4. Because poles can dissipate wind loading directly into the ground, a pole structure can weather intense storms and flooding that would damage a conventional building.

Wood beams are remarkably resistant to fire. Here a charred wooden beam continues to support two steel I-beams that have melted and collapsed due to the heat of the fire.

Versatility

The pole building advantages of low cost, simple foundation systems, and framing flexibility make this type of construction well suited to a wide variety of structures. Barns, garages, and utility buildings are ideal candidates for pole construction where strength and economy are the main concern. Pole construction also offers a solution to building a cabin or vacation home at a remote site that is inaccessible or impractical to reach with heavy equipment. And for normal residential construction, pole building can overcome the limitations of slopes and poor soils at the building site.

The notion that pole building is a last resort, suitable only for non-permanent structures, is finally disappearing; pole-framed structures of every kind imaginable — barns, houses, office buildings, and churches — are being built. In an era of rising costs of labor, materials, and land, pole building's versatility and economy will ensure that this trend continues.

POLE BUILDING DESIGN

CHAPTER TWO

To take advantage of the inherent flexibilities and economies of pole building requires a carefully considered design and plan. There are four principal considerations that must be addressed before starting construction: site selection, framing design, functional design, and materials.

Site Selection

Perhaps the greatest advantage of pole building, aside from cost, is that you can build without disturbing the natural environment of a site. You can build in a dense forest setting without clearcutting a large area, you can build on a steep hillside without disturbing the vegetation and causing erosion, and you can build on wet soils without altering drainage patterns.

Topography and Soils

The topography of a site is the first thing to look at. In general, the greater the slope of the land, the harder it is to build and control erosion. Thus, a flat site is usually preferable to a steep one, especially if there is going to be a road and parking area. But because pole foundations are easily adapted to steep slopes, hillside con-

Figure 2-1. Topographical factors that influence building site selection.

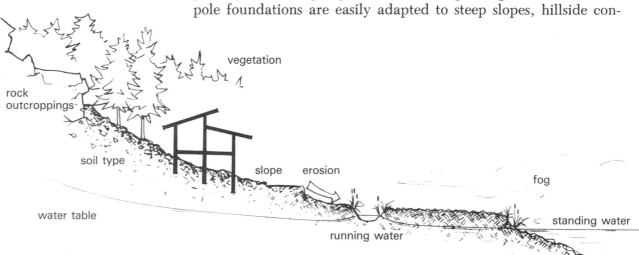

struction also can offer some advantages. By building on a slope, land costs can often be reduced, winter winds can be buffered by the hillside, flooding and drainage problems avoided, flatter land on a piece of property can be saved for gardening or farming, and good views opened up.

Soil characteristics are the next consideration and are very important in terms of pole embedment depth and load carrying capacity. There are three main inorganic components of soil which determine its strength and drainage characteristics: sand, silt, and clay. Table 2–1 lists the characteristics of soils with different percentages of these materials. As can be seen, gravelly and sandy soils are much better for building than clay soils. When selecting a site, keep in mind that pole buildings can be put up on almost any type of soil but that foundations will be more complicated and expensive as soil quality decreases.

The American Wood Preservers Institute (AWPI) has devised a classification of three soil types—good, average, and below average—along with accompanying tables for pole embedment depth. Their recommendations are the best for the owner-builder to follow. This method of determining pole embedment depth is presented in detail in chapter 5.

Table 2–1

RATINGS FOR VARIOUS SOIL TYPES

Typical Name for Soil Type	General Characteristics			Fill Soil							Undistorted Soil		
				Special Characteristics				Use			Foundation		
				Ability to Compact	Hydrologic Reaction			Foundation	Drain	Frost	Dense Hard	Loose Soft	Drainage
	Stability	Permeability	Corrosion Potential		Pack	Expand	Frost						
Bedrock	Ex	NS	Ex	VP	NS	NS	VP	Ex	NS	VP	Ex	Ex	NS
Coarse Grain													
Gravel	Ex	Ex	Ex	Ex	Ex	VP	Ex	Ex	Ex	Ex	Ex	Ex	Ex
Gravel/Sand	VG	VG	Ex	VG	Ex	VP	Ex	VG	Ex	G	Ex	NS	Ex
Gravel/Silt	Med	G-P	Ex	G	VG	P	G-Ex	G	VG	G-VG	VG	VG	VG
Gravel/Clay	F	VP	VG	G	G	F	G-VG	G	VG	F-Med	G	Ex	VG
Sand	G	Ex	Ex	Ex	Ex	VP	Ex	VG	Ex	VG-Med	Ex	VG-Ex	Ex
Sand/Silt	F-G	G-P	Ex	G	G	F	G	G	Ex	F-VP	VG	VG	VG
Sand/Clay	F	VP	VG	G	G	F	G	Med	NS	F	G	VG	VG
Fine Grain													
Clay/Silt	P	G-P	VG	F-G	G	F	G-Med	F	NS	P-VP	G	G	VG
Clay	P	VP	G	G	Med	Med	G	F	NS	F-P	G-VP	G-Med	VG
Organic Silt	P	G-P	G	F	F	G	G	P	NS	P-VP	G-VP	G	VG
Inorganic Silt	P	G-P	VG	F-G	F	G	G-Med	VP	NS	VP	Med	G	VG
Inorganic Clay	VP	VP	G	F-G	F	G	G	P	NS	VP-F	Med-P	G-VG	NS
Organic Clay	VP	VP	G	F	F	G	G	VP	NS	VP	F-VP	Med	NS
Loam	NS	NS	Med	NS	NS	NS	VG	NS	NS	NS	F	NS	NS

(From: FHA BULLETIN No. 373.)

RATINGS: Ex-Excellent, VG-Very Good, G-Good, Med-Medium, F-Fair, P-Poor, VP-Very Poor, NS-Not Suitable to use.

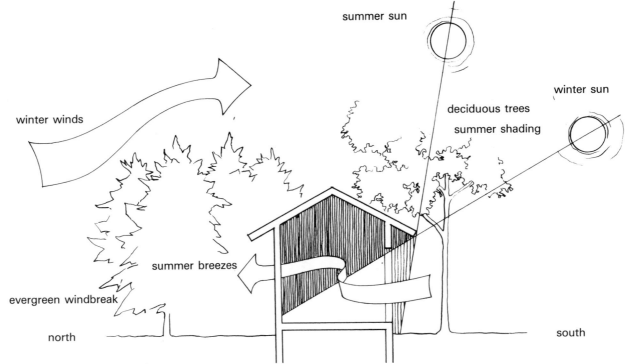

summer sun

winter sun

deciduous trees

summer shading

winter winds

summer breezes

evergreen windbreak

north

south

Figure 2-2. Building orientation with respect to the sun and seasonal breezes greatly effects comfort and energy efficiency.

Orientation

In terms of energy conservation, building orientation is very important and should be considered during site selection. Sun, shading, and prevailing winds are three factors that will determine year-round comfort.

In northern climates, proper use of a southern exposure is very important. South-facing buildings should take advantage of passive solar heating oportunities by having the majority of the windows on the south side. This dramatically reduces winter fuel bills. A southern exposure also provides natural daylighting, making any building more pleasant and energy-efficient. Remember, the sun is very low in the sky during the winter, so be sure that trees and other obstructions won't block the sun during these often dreary months. Appendix D lists the lowest and highest sun angles throughout the year for various latitudes.

Summer shading can be just as important as winter heating especially in southern climates. Summer shading can be provided by deciduous trees that are leafed out in summer but bare in winter to let the sunlight through when you want it. Roof and window overhangs are another way to achieve summer shading. These should be considered in your building design.

Consideration of the prevailing winds is important for winter warmth and summer cooling. The winter winds are normally from the north, and therefore a south facing building on a south facing hillside is often ideal for protection. In a similar manner, a building can be oriented to take advantage of summer breezes for cooling in hot climates.

Looking at a Site

When looking over a possible building site you will want to determine the general slopes and soil characteristics. The tools you should have are a post hole digger, a level, a compass, a length of string, and two stakes.

First, take some compass readings to find north and south. Make a quick sketch of the building site using landmarks such as trees, rocks, or other buildings and mark the compass directions on the sketch.

To measure slopes, use the two stakes, a ten-foot length of string, and the level. At the top of a slope, drive one stake and tie the string to it at ground level. Loop the other end of the ten-foot string around the other stake and stretch it downhill until it is taut. Level the string by holding the level to it, and then measure the height from the string to the ground. If the string is 12 inches off the ground then the slope in that area is 1:10. Take a compass reading along the direction of the slope and mark that on your map with the slope ratio. This information will be useful when determining your pole embedment depth and the length of poles that you need.

To determine soil characteristics, dig several test holes around the building site. The holes should be several feet deep or deep enough to show a complete soil profile of the various layers of soil. A normal soil profile will contain several inches of topsoil that is high in organic matter, a deeper layer of subsoil that is composed of sand, silt, and clay, and then a layer of substratum that is unweathered rock and gravel. The subsoil is the part that interests us most in terms of a pole foundation. A friable, well-drained subsoil that has a high sand content makes for an excellent foundation soil. A clumpy, wet soil that has a high clay content is less desireable. Table 2–1 presents a soil classification chart which shows the characteristics of different types of soils.

Zoning and Building Codes

Another factor in site selection is zoning laws. Most land in the United States is now zoned for certain uses. Make sure the building you are considering meets the zoning requirements for permitted uses, setbacks from property lines, and type of structure.

In heavily regulated urban and suburban areas, the local planning commission may at first feel that a pole building (especially if it is the first one they've seen) is out of keeping with the architectural style of the area. It should take very little time, however, to convince them that your pole building can be built and dressed up to match any kind of style they demand. When the poles are set within the building shell, it is very difficult indeed to tell that a house sits on a pole foundation, unless you choose to emphasize this in your design. Thus you can accomodate design restrictions if necessary, and still have a pole building.

Building codes are another hurdle for many owner-builders. While pole building was originally frowned on by building inspectors, it has more than proven itself to meet all applicable structural and safety requirements. In fact, pole buildings are more fire resistant, more flood proof, and more hurricane proof than conventional buildings. In many townships that get periodic flooding, high winds, or mudslides, pole construction is now required by law.

Pole building is now heartily endorsed and promoted by the Federal Housing Authority and receiving a building permit for a well-designed pole structure should be no more difficult than getting one for a conventional structure.

Framing Design

There are two principal methods of pole building, pole framing and platform framing. *Pole framing* utilizes poles for foundation, wall, and roof support. In essence, the building is hung on a framework of poles. *Platform framing* uses a pole foundation to support a conventional platform and stud-framed structure.

Pole vs. Platform Framing

While both methods utilize poles as a low cost foundation, pole framing has several added advantages. It has superior structural strength in the face of hurricanes, floods, and earthquakes because the poles support and tie together the entire structure, absorbing and transmitting these forces into the ground. Because floors and the roof are supported independently by the poles, there is great flexibility in wall and window placement. The size of poles, their spacing, and the depth of embedment are all important to the structural integrity of a pole-framed building. These are covered in detail in chapters 5 and 6.

Platform framing has the advantage of simplicity and conventional construction methods. For the owner-builder who is trying to build a two-story pole house all by his or herself, platform framing might be the only option available. A twenty-foot pole can weigh well over 500 pounds and be mighty hard to muscle into place with three people, let alone single-handedly. Because platform framing uses individual small studs and joists to frame walls and floors, one person can frame an entire building alone. Contractors are also usually much more familiar with platform framing, and may be willing to put in a pole foundation but not frame with poles.

Pole Framing Terms

The parts of a pole framed building are shown in figure 2–3. The frame is built on to round poles or square posts that are usually

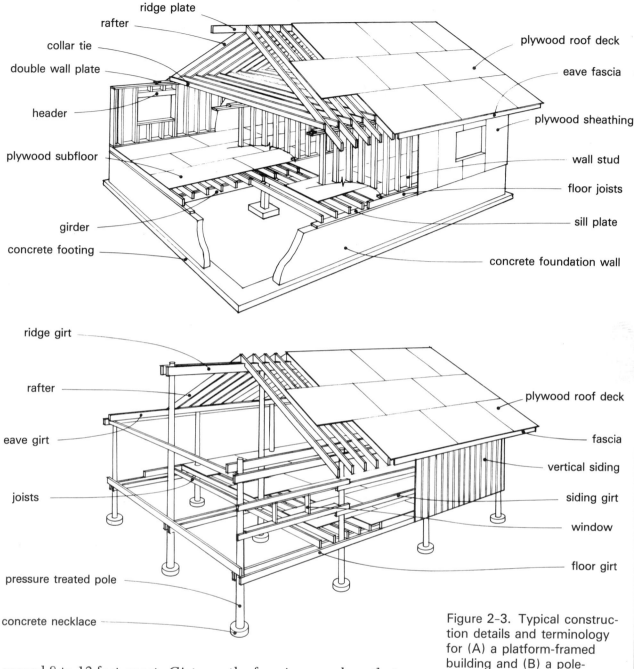

ridge plate
rafter
collar tie
double wall plate
header
plywood subfloor
girder
concrete footing

plywood roof deck
eave fascia
plywood sheathing
wall stud
floor joists
sill plate
concrete foundation wall

ridge girt
rafter
eave girt
joists
pressure treated pole
concrete necklace

plywood roof deck
fascia
vertical siding
siding girt
window
floor girt

Figure 2–3. Typical construction details and terminology for (A) a platform-framed building and (B) a pole-framed building.

spaced 8 to 12 feet apart. *Girts* are the framing members that span between the poles to carry the floors, walls, and roof of a building.

Starting from the bottom up, there is the *sill girt* which is the bottom nailer for the siding and extends into the ground to close off the bottom of the building. The sill girt uses 2×10 pressure-treated lumber so it won't rot, and so there is an adequate splash area below the siding. The *floor girts* are next, and these are usually double 2×10s or 2×12s to support the weight of the floor joists which rest on them. *Siding girts* are nailed on the outside of the poles, 24 inches on center (o.c.) as a nail base for the siding. These are usually 2×4s or 2×6s since they only carry the weight of the siding. At the top of the poles are *rafter girts* which are again usually double 2 × 10s or 2 × 12s that support the roof rafters. Sometimes there are two sets of girts that support the rafters, an *eave girt* at the bottom and a *ridge girt* at the top.

All the other framing members are the same as in conventional platform construction. Walls are framed with 2 × 4 or 2 × 6 *studs*, floors with 2 × 6 or larger *joists*, and roofs with 2 × 6 or larger *rafters*. Chapter 4 discusses in detail how to size all these framing members based on the building design and the distance each member spans.

Pole Placement

In general, the owner-builder will find pole framing to be the preferred method of building because of its strength, low material cost, and suitability for cabins, barns, and outbuildings. Figures 2–4 to 2–6 show several different pole framing arrangements with the poles outside, in, and inside the walls.

Leaving the poles on the outside of the walls is common for pole house construction where the walls must be plumb, finished on both sides, and airtight. With this construction method, the

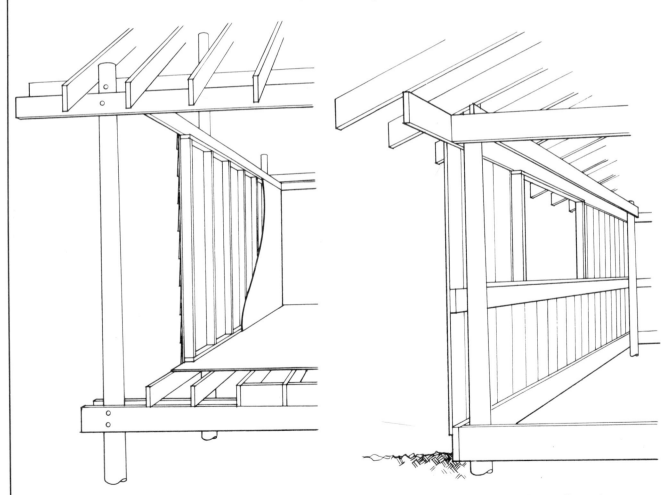

Figure 2-4. A pole house with the foundation poles outside conventionally framed 2 × 6 walls.

Figure 2-5. A pole barn with the walls and siding hung directly on the poles.

poles are not in the way of the siding and interior finish, no preservatives or odor are inside the house shell, and the poles are accessible, so they can be replaced if they ever fail in the future.

For barn construction, poles are often in the wall since there is no interior wall finish or floor, and the poles simply need to support a roof and the siding. In this case, the poles are plumbed on the outside to give a vertical wall, as their taper on the inside doesn't matter. If the barn is to be insulated, 2×4 girt braces are simply framed between the poles to hold the insulation (see figure 6–19).

A final way to frame is with the poles visible on the inside of the walls. This has two advantages. The poles are not visible from the outside and thus a pole house can masquerade as a conventional structure to meet aesthetic goals or design restrictions. The floors can also cantilever beyond the poles, increasing the square footage of a house without increasing foundation size. The major drawback to this method is that the poles take up room inside the structure and bring toxic preservatives inside. The poles can, however, be satisfactorily boxed and finished to effectively seal them off.

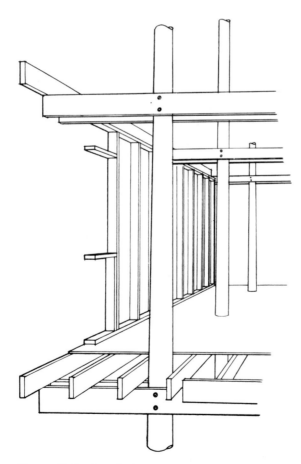

Figure 2-6. A pole house with the poles inside of the building. Notice how the floor girts are cantilevered past the poles.

Roof Styles

One thing you might have noticed already about pole buildings is that all the roof framing is the same, conventional rafter framing. Because of this, any type of roof can be put on top of a pole structure. Gable, hip, shed, and gambrel roofs are common types for pole buildings, each with its own advantages.

A *gable roof* has two equally pitched sides and is one of the easiest roof configurations to frame. Steeply pitched gables are well suited to northern climates because they shed snow and are easily insulated and ventilated. A variation on the gable is a salt box roof that has two unequal pitches and is useful for expanding the southern exposure of a passive solar house or simply opening up a house to the best views.

A *hip roof* has four sides and is slightly more complicated to frame. It is an attractive roof for single-story structures, as it eliminates the gable end walls and eave details, saving time and money.

The *shed roof* is a single straight pitched roof often found on small barns and outbuildings. It is the simplest type to frame and simply requires the front wall to be higher than the rear wall to give the roof some pitch. This is also its limiting factor in that the pitch is usually never great enough to shed snow. Therefore, such roofs must be carefully designed and built to withstand large snow loads in northern climates.

Gambrel roofs are often found on barns where they serve to give more head height and storage room on the top floor. They are, of course, harder to frame but they can make the top story of a house or barn much more useful and add a distinctive touch to the building's style.

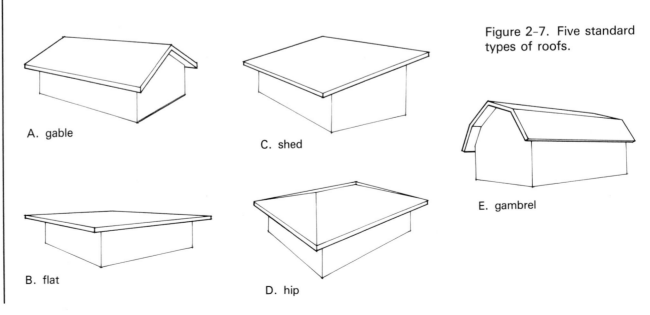

Figure 2-7. Five standard types of roofs.

A. gable

C. shed

B. flat

D. hip

E. gambrel

Functional Design

Functional design involves anticipating all the uses you want a building to perform and then designing the building around these uses in a logical and efficient way. This kind of design is no less important for a barn than it is for a house. A barn may be much easier to design because it serves fewer functions, but it still must have some thought put into it, so the horses fit into the stalls and the hay into the hayloft.

The Activity List

The first step in designing a building is to make a detailed list of all the activities that might possibly go on in the building. The activities should be annotated with notes that describe details of the activities that might be important to design.

Figure 2–8 is an activity list for the pole cabin that is presented in Part 2 of this book. A quick look at this list shows that it is as inclusive and specific as possible. The loft area is one example. Every house, of course, needs a sleeping area, but in the case of the pole cabin there are no beds, just sleeping bags on mattresses. Therefore, a small loft area would be ideal for combined sleeping and storage and would eliminate the need to divide the already small cabin into separate rooms.

It also is important to indicate the dimensions and sometimes weight of appliances or equipment that will be used. Our pole cabin will be using a wood stove for heating, which means that we can cook on it and thereby save counter space in the kitchen. We can use a small gas burner unit for cooking in the summer, but we'll need to know how big it is so we can design a space for it in the kitchen.

Dimensions and weights are especially critical for barn planning. How many cubic feet do 8 tons of grain take up? Is that tractor 12 or 14 feet long? A detailed inventory of equipment and storage requirements is a prerequisite for a successful building. (See appendix H for measurements of commonly used equipment.)

The Floor Plan

The next step in the design process is to take your activity list and make a *schematic drawing* from it. The first drawing should be just a series of circles with the activities in them and connecting lines showing which activities are interconnected and how the flow of movement in a building will take place. Figure 2–9 shows this type of drawing for our pole cabin and helps us visualize which activities are most important and central to the use of the building.

This schematic drawing can then be used to do a rough sketch

Figure 2-8. The first step in building design is to draw up an Activity List of everything that will happen inside and outside of the building.

POLE CABIN ACTIVITY LIST

Eating

Storage
Cooking
Eating
Washing
Cook Stove

Living

Sitting
Reading
Music
Views
Writing
Talking
Playing

Sleeping

Storage
Sleeping
Guest Room

Bathing

Toilet
Washing
Sauna

Miscellaneous

Storing Wood
Hammock/Deck Chairs
Waxing Skis
Storing Equipment

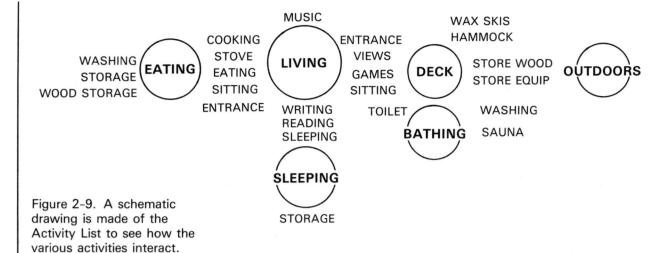

Figure 2-9. A schematic drawing is made of the Activity List to see how the various activities interact.

of a floor plan that hopefully will optimize the spatial relationship between all the activities. Our cabin design is very simple, being one large room, but there are quite a few design decisions that have gone into its layout.

Traffic flow. A major consideration is traffic flow, how people move from one activity to another. In the cabin, the entrances are aligned so people can move through the cabin without interrupting work in the kitchen or people sitting by the stove. The kitchen is tucked into the back corner to minimize the distance between sink, stove, and refrigerator. The rap-around porch covered

Figure 2-10. The final stage of design is a floor plan that attempts to arrange the building elements in an efficient and aesthetically pleasing way. Shown here is the pole cabin floor plan from Part 2.

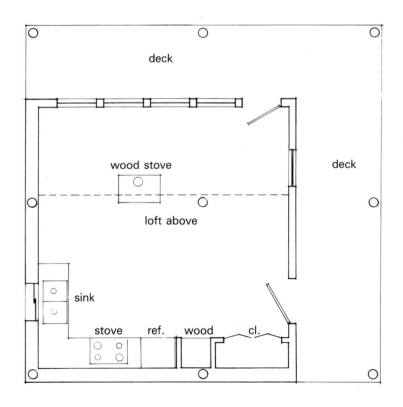

by an overhanging roof is another design feature that will allow ski and hiking equipment to be kept outside, as well as some activities, minimizing disruption of the inside living area.

Appeal. Comfort and visual appeal are two other guiding factors in the floor plan. The living area is placed on the south next to the glass wall which lets in light and heat, making it a very pleasant area for relaxing. This also provides good views from the living area. A skylight on the south roof lets in light and heat to the loft area, and in the summer will provide ventilation.

Energy. Energy conservation is also important. The north wall has no windows, since little light would come in from this side anyway, and a great deal of heat would be lost. This works perfectly with the kitchen placement, since we would have to sacrifice wall cabinets and storage to put in windows. Even the woodbox, located next to the outer door, is there for the purpose of minimizing the time the outer door is open, and the amount of snow and wood debris that gets tracked inside.

An Integrated Design

With a rough floor plan, we are ready to proceed to the next step, framing design. The framing design should indicate what size poles are being used, what their spacing is, the size of supporting girts, joists, and rafters. Chapter 4 presents in detail a simple method for calculating these factors.

Now is the time to consider what materials to use. Your choice of siding, roofing, windows, and doors will have a big impact on the aesthetics of your pole building, as well as your budget. Chapter 3 discusses poles and framing material, and chapters 7 and 8 outline different siding, roofing, window, and door options.

To finalize your building design, you need to consider all of the factors that we have discussed, from functional design to framing design to aesthetic design. You will find that they all interact and influence one another.

Structural considerations, for example, might force you to move your poles closer together; this, in turn, will change the dimensions of your floor plan, which might mean you can't put the kitchen where you thought. Back to the drawing board! You'll find this kind of creative integration—trying to put together all the requirements for your building—will guide you to a better understanding of how your building can meet for your needs in the most efficient way.

Some Special Pole Building Details

Bringing water, sewer, and electricity into a pole building often causes some confusion because of the lack of basement foundation and less familiar framing techniques. Insulating pole buildings and their foundations is another detail that raises questions. It is important to think these details through before finalizing a particular design and certainly before starting construction.

Insulation

Pole buildings can be insulated as well as, if not better than, conventional structures. Because the pole frame supports the floors and the roof, the walls are non-loadbearing and therefore can be framed with less wood and more insulation.

Choosing the Right Insulation

There are many different types of insulation and picking the right one for the job often requires some thought. There are three basic categories of insulation: loose fill, blankets, and rigid boards.

Loose fills are made from fiberglass, rock wool, cellulose (paper fiber), and vermiculite (expanded mica). These are blown in place or poured from a bag. Cellulose is the most widely used loose fill, often used to insulate attics and walls of older houses where the wall and ceiling finish is already in place.

Blankets are made from fiberglass in various thicknesses and widths. This type of insulation is widely used for walls and ceilings in new construction because of its relatively low cost and ease of installation. Blankets come in widths of 15 inches and 23 inches to fit between studs 16 and 24 inches on center (o.c.), respectively. Thicknesses range from 3½ inches to 12 inches. The blankets come unfaced or faced with a kraft paper or foil backing. Use unfaced since it is the least expensive. If it must be stapled to hold it in place, then choose kraft-faced. Foil-backed insulation is more expensive and unnecessary for normal residential construction.

Rigid boards are made from various types of foam. Blueboard or pinkboard made from extruded polystyrene is used to insulate foundations. It is not damaged by moisture or contact with the ground, but must be protected from the sun. Blueboard has twice the R value of fiberglass per inch of thickness but it is about four times as expensive per R value. Polyisocyanurate foam sold under brand names such as "Thermax" and "Hi-R" has even a higher R value per inch. It is used as a sheathing on walls and attic rafters to boost the insulation where there is not enough space for an adequate amount of fiberglass. For example, on a roof with 2×8 rafters only 6 inches of fiberglass can be put between the rafters still leaving a 1-inch ventilation space under the roof deck. Two inches of foam could be nailed on the underside of the rafters to almost double the R value of the roof system. Because of its high cost, however, rigid foam boards should only be used where fiberglass won't work because of space limitations or moisture conditions.

Appendix F lists all the different types of insulation, their relative costs, and uses.

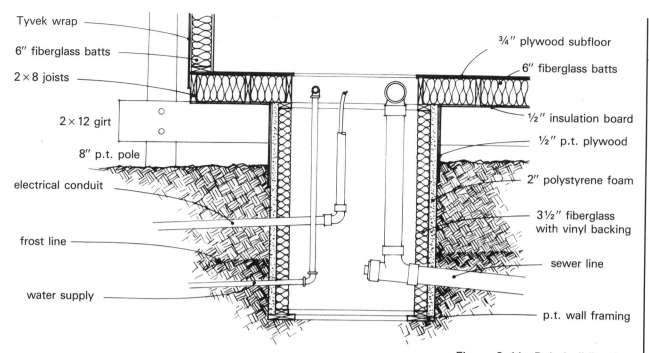

Tyvek wrap
6" fiberglass batts
2 × 8 joists
2 × 12 girt
8" p.t. pole
electrical conduit
frost line
water supply

¾" plywood subfloor
6" fiberglass batts
½" insulation board
½" p.t. plywood
2" polystyrene foam
3½" fiberglass with vinyl backing
sewer line
p.t. wall framing

Figure 2-11. Pole building insulation details showing an insulated chase for bringing in electrical, water, and sewer lines.

Figure 2–11 shows a typical pole house with 6 inches of fiberglass in the floor, 6 inches in the walls, and 12 inches in the ceiling. There is also a polyethylene *vapor barrier* on all the exterior walls and the attic ceiling to prevent interior house moisture from entering the insulation and then condensing along the cold outer wall surface. Vapor barriers are extremely important in cold climates to keep insulation dry and effective, and also to protect the framing from moisture build up and rot. Notice that because the underside of the house is open, the floor must be well insulated. Also, the water and utility lines coming into the house are located in an insulated pipe chase.

Panel construction. Pole building is very suitable for using pre-manufactured panel construction. In this case, 4 × 8 panels consisting of a foam core sandwiched between ½-inch waferboard on the exterior and ½-inch drywall on the interior are nailed directly on to the poles. Panels with either 3½-inch foam cores (R-value = 16) or 5½-inch cores (R-value = 26) are available to fit standard window and door jamb thicknesses. Laminated panel construction forms a very tight wall surface with a high R-value because there is no wood framing to interrupt the insulation. It also allows the sheathing, insulation, and interior drywall to go on all at once, cutting labor costs dramatically.

Because of these advantages, panel construction has become a popular choice of contractors who build post and beam, and pole houses. Compared on a materials basis, laminated panel construction is about 50 percent more expensive than conventional wall framing, but it provides a much tighter, high R-value wall at a fraction of the labor cost.

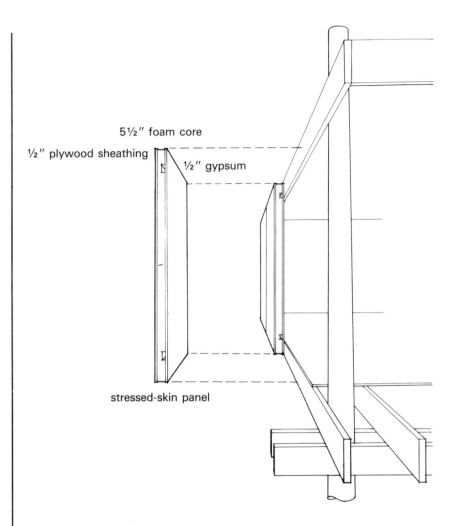

5½″ foam core

½″ plywood sheathing

½″ gypsum

stressed-skin panel

Figure 2-12. The labor economy and energy-efficiency of foam core stressed-skin panels are revolutionizing the building industry.

Insulated skirts. For pole buildings that have the floor slightly elevated off the ground, it is often desirable to install an insulated skirt around the perimeter of the building to close off the crawl space. This not only helps insulate the building, but can keep out animals that might try to nest under the house. A skirt can be made of 2-inch polystyrene foam nailed to the poles, or to special skirt framing. It should extend from the bottom of the floor and be bur-

Figure 2-13. An insulated skirt is often desireable to close off the crawl space under pole buildings.

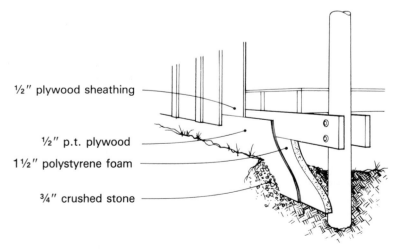

½″ plywood sheathing

½″ p.t. plywood

1½″ polystyrene foam

¾″ crushed stone

ied in the earth several inches. The foam can then be covered with either a fiberglass reinforced stucco mixture or pressure-treated plywood to protect the foam from damage by sunlight or animals. Small operable vents should be installed in the foam to allow summer ventilation to remove excess moisture. Chapter 7 has further details on installing insulated skirts.

Plumbing and Electrical Systems

Plumbing and heating systems are normally placed in the basement of conventional structures and then run up through the house walls. Since pole buildings have no basement, it is necessary to plan for a utility closet on the first floor that can hold the heating system, water tank, and electrical service panel. Often it is wise to locate this utility area in the center of a building to minimize pipe, duct, and wire runs.

A major problem encountered in pole building is how to bring in water and sewer lines to a house without a basement. The best way is to design an *insulated pipe chase* that can bring a ¾-inch water line, 4-inch sewer pipe, and electrical service into the house from one central location underneath. A 12-inch square pressure-treated box with 2 inches of foam insulation on the outside works well. The box is buried in the earth below the frost line, insulated the entire length, and then left open inside the house to provide a source of heat to keep the pipes warm in winter. In severe northern climates, a small piece of heat tape may be necessary to keep the box warm during the dead of winter. Usually, however, the warmth of the earth, the house, and the insulation is all that is needed.

Once inside the structure, running plumbing or wiring is no more difficult than in a conventional building. It is always wise, however, to minimize plumbing and wiring in the exterior walls where it reduces the effectiveness of insulation and vapor barriers. Try to keep your plumbing and wiring runs accessible, such as in a chase in the back of a closet, for future renovations and additions. If something goes wrong or you need to add an outlet, you know where to look and don't have to tear open finished walls.

If you are using laminated foam panels, these usually have pre-made channels at the top and bottom for running wiring around the walls. If a channel is not being used for wiring, it could be used for flexible water supply piping since the channel is big enough and also insulated from the exterior wall surface.

One way to keep wiring and plumbing out of walls is to build a special baseboard that doubles as a chase. Figure 2–14 shows such a baseboard that can handle electrical wiring and outlets without penetrating the vapor barrier and wall insulation.

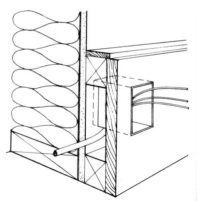

Figure 2-14. Electrical boxes can be a large source of heat loss in newly constructed buildings. Here's a baseboard detail that allows you to run wiring without disturbing the insulation or penetrating the vapor barrier.

Chimneys

Wood, gas, or oil heating systems must all have a chimney or flue to exhaust combustion gases. There are two choices for chimneys in a pole building, a masonry chimney or a metal-asbestos chimney.

A masonry chimney built of concrete block or brick with flue tile running up the center is both durable and attractive. Because of its large weight, however, such a chimney requires its own foundation. This is usually a concrete footing slightly larger than the chimney itself, poured down below the frost line.

A less expensive and less labor intensive alternative is to install a metal-asbestos chimney. These are insulated stainless steel chimneys that can be run directly from a wood stove or heating system through floors and walls and out the roof. The chimney comes in 3-foot sections that interlock and can be hung with brackets from the house framing. The stainless steel flue itself is very expensive, but requires no foundation and very little labor to install. Thus, for most pole buildings, it would be the most economical chimney system.

Pouring Concrete Floors

For pole barns, warehouses, or garages, it is often desireable to have a concrete floor for animals or vehicles. Dirt and gravel floors are inexpensive, but they are hard to clean and maintain.

Because there are no foundation walls in a pole building, a reinforced, floating slab must be poured inside of the poles. It is called a *floating slab* because it is independent of the building's foundation. This allows it to move in response to changes in temperature and frost without putting pressure on the pole foundation.

Figure 2-15 details the construction of a floating slab with thickened edges and heavy metal reinforcements to keep it from cracking as it moves. Notice the 1-inch foam expansion joint around the perimeter which isolates it from the wall framing.

Figure 2-15. Concrete floating slab detail.

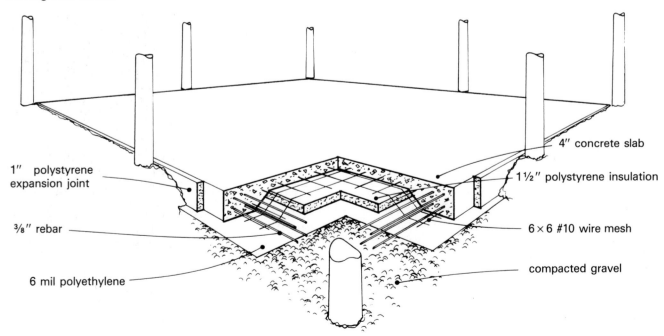

1″ polystyrene expansion joint

3/8″ rebar

6 mil polyethylene

4″ concrete slab

1½″ polystyrene insulation

6 × 6 #10 wire mesh

compacted gravel

POLES AND FRAMING MATERIALS

Pole building is set apart from conventional wood framing by the use of an interlocking framework of poles and supporting girts which carry all of a building's loads. Roof, siding, and flooring details are all fairly similar to conventional framing.

Because of the unique loadbearing function of poles and girts, it is important that they be selected carefully. The poles are in contact with the ground, and therefore they must be treated with a wood preservative if they are to last. There are several different types of wood preservatives with different characteristics. Girts should be selected on the basis of their strength, which varies greatly between species of wood, and how the lumber has been processed. And, of course, there is always the matter of your building budget to contend with.

This chapter looks into the details of selecting poles and girts based on these and other factors.

Foundation Poles and Posts

There are several different types of round poles or square timbers you can use for pole building. The choice will depend on what kind of structure you are building, how much money you can spend, and the local availability of different types of poles. Telephone poles, pressure-treated with a preservative, are most commonly used for large, permanent structures since they are strong, rot resistant and come in lengths from 20 to over 100 feet long. Pressure-treated timbers such as 6 × 6s and 8 × 8s can also be used for small buildings under 12 feet tall and are readily available at most lumberyards. If pressure-treated poles are not available, untreated poles cut from locally available trees can be used for semi-permanent structures.

The necessity of preservative treatment for poles that are in contact with the earth should not be underestimated. An untreated pole, even if made from a highly decay-resistant wood species such as cedar, will probably last only 10 years once buried in the ground in a moist environment. A less resistant species such as hemlock will have an even shorter life span. A pressure-treated pole, however, should last 50 years or longer given modern pressure-treating methods.

A pole yard with piles sorted according to pole class, length, and preservative treatment.

Every pole is stamped to indicate the type of wood species, preservative treatment, class, and pole length.

Pressure-treated Poles

Pressure-treated poles are widely used by utilities, railroads, and billboard companies and are available in almost every part of the United States. These poles are classified by standards set by the American Wood Preservers Association (AWPA) as to minimum diameter and length. There are 10 classes of poles, each with a minimum top and bottom circumference, depending on the length of the pole. Table 3–1 lists these classes and their minimum dimensions.

Poles are usually cut from four recommended species of trees: southern, red, and ponderosa pines, and Pacific coast Douglas fir. These species have a high fiber stress rating and are generally very straight.

Table 3–1

POLE CLASSES

Class	1	2	3	4	5	6	7	9	10
Diameter at Top (Inches)	8½	8	7¼	6¾	6	5½	4¾	4¾	4¼
Minimum Circumference at Top (Inches)	27	25	23	21	19	17	15	15	12
Length of Pole (Feet)	Minimum Circumference at 6 Feet from Butt (Inches)								
20	31.0	29.0	27.0	25.0	23.0	**21.0**	**19.5**	**17.5**	**14.0**
25	33.5	31.5	29.5	27.5	25.5	**23.0**	**21.5**	**19.5**	**15.0**
30	36.5	**34.0**	**32.0**	**29.5**	**27.5**	25.0	23.5	20.5	
35	39.0	**36.5**	**34.0**	**31.5**	**29.0**	**27.0**	25.0		
40	**41.0**	**38.5**	**36.0**	**33.5**	**31.0**	**28.5**	26.5		
45	**43.0**	**40.5**	**37.5**	**35.0**	**32.5**	30.0	28.0		
50	**45.0**	**42.0**	**39.0**	36.5	34.0	31.5	29.0		
55	**46.5**	**43.5**	**40.5**	38.0	35.0	32.5			
60	**48.0**	**45.0**	**42.0**	39.0	36.0	33.5			
65	**49.5**	**46.5**	**43.5**	40.5	37.5				
70	**51.0**	**48.0**	**45.0**	41.5	38.5				
75	**52.5**	**49.0**	**46.0**	43.0					
80	**54.0**	**50.5**	47.0	44.0					
85	**55.0**	**51.5**	48.0						
90	**56.0**	**53.0**	49.0						
95	**57.0**	**54.0**	50.0						
100	**58.5**	**55.0**	51.0						
105	**59.5**	**56.0**	52.0						
110	**60.5**	**57.0**	53.0						
115	**61.5**	**58.0**							
120	**62.5**	**59.0**							
125	**63.5**	**59.5**							

Note: Preferred standard sizes are those listed in boldface type. Those shown in light type are included for engineering purposes only.
(From: Donald Patterson, Pole Building Design. McLean, Virginia: AWPI, 1969.)

Pressure-treated utility poles are commonly used for most large pole building projects.

Preservative Treatments

There are three principal types of preservative chemicals that are used: pentachlorophenol, water-borne salts, and creosote. The choice of preservative is very important in terms of pole appearance, paintability, cleanliness, and odor. All preservatives are injected into the wood under pressure to give a minimum penetration of 2½ inches and a certain retention measured in pounds per cubic foot. Table 3–2 lists the various AWPA standards for preservative treatment.

Pentachlorophenol is perhaps the most commonly used preservative as it imparts little color or odor and is highly resistant to leaching. It is applied in solution with either a heavy oil, a light petroleum solvent, or in a liquid petroleum gas. The heavy oil treatment (common on telephone poles) leaves an oily residue that cannot be painted, which makes it undesireable for building. For pole building, the light solvent process (AWPI LP-3) or the gas process (AWPI LP-4) is preferable, especially if the poles are to be painted.

Table 3–2

RECOMMENDED PRESERVATIVES AND RETENTIONS

	Water-Borne Preservatives[1,2]					Oil-Borne[3]		
	Chromated copper arsenate (CCA-Types A, B, C)	Ammoniacal copper arsenate (ACA)	Acid copper chromate (ACC)	Chromated Zinc chloride (CZC)	Fluor chrome arsenate phenol (FCAP)	Pentachlorophenol[3]	Creosote & creosote-coal tar	AWPA Stan
AWPA Preservative Standard				AWPA Standard				
Product & Use	Minimum Net Retention in lbs./cu. ft.[4]							
Lumber and timber								
Above ground	0.25	0.25	0.25	0.46	0.22	0.40	8	C2
Soil or fresh water contact								
Non-structural	0.40	0.40	0.50	NR[5]	NR	0.50	10	C2
Structural-foundations, bridges, etc.	0.60	0.60	NR	NR	NR	0.60	12	C14
In salt water	2.5	2.5	NR	NR	NR	NR	25	C14
Plywood								
Above ground	0.25	0.25	0.25	0.46	0.22	0.40	8	C9
Soil or fresh water contact	0.40	0.40	0.50	NR	NR	0.50	10	C9
Piles								
Soil or fresh water use and foundations	0.80	0.80	NR	NR	NR	0.60	12	C3
In salt water								
Severe borer hazard— Limnoria[6]	2.5[8] & 1.5	2.5[8] & 1.5	NR	NR	NR	NR	NR	C18
Moderate borer hazard— Pholads[7]	NR	NR	NR	NR	NR	NR	20	C18
For both Pholads and Limnoria a dual treatment can be specified								
First treatment	1.0	1.0	NR	NR	NR	NR	—	C18
Second treatment	—	—	NR	NR	NR	NR	20	C18
Poles								
Utility								
Normal service conditions	0.60	0.60	NR	NR	NR	0.38	7.5	C4
Severe decay & termite areas	0.60	0.60	NR	NR	NR	0.45	9.0	C4
Building poles—structural	0.60	0.60	NR	NR	NR	0.45	9.0	C23

Source: Society of American Wood Preservers.

1 Trade names of water-borne preservatives: Chromated Copper Arsenate (CCA) (Type A); Greensalt, Langwood; (Type B) Boliden CCA; Koppers CCA-B; Osmose K-33; (Type C) Chrom-Ar-Cu (CAC); Osmose K-33 C; Wolman* CCA; Wolmanac CCA; Ammoniacal Copper Arsenate (ACA); Chemonite Acide Copper Chromate (ACC); Celcure Chromated Zinc Chloride (CZC); none Fluor Chrome Arsenate Phenol (FCAP); Osmosalts* (Osmosar*); Tanalith; Wolman FCAP; Wolman FMP.

2 Where cleanliness, paintability or odor are factors, and in certain salt-water areas, the approved water-borne preservatives should be used. Creosote, creosote-coal tar solution, and oil-borne penta are not recommended in these cases.

3 Penta in light or water-repellent solvents, and liquid petroleum gas carriers can provide clean, paintable surfaces. The processor should be advised when painting after treatment is intended.

4 AWPA Standard CI applies to all process and types of materials. Minimum net retentions in this chart conform to AWPA standards for all softwood species in the cases of lumber and plywood. Retentions for piles, poles and posts are based on AWPA Standards for southern pine. When other species are used for these items, AWPA requires different retentions. All water-borne retentions are oxide basis.

5 NR—Not recommended.

6 Limnoria Tripunctata are usually the most destructive marine borers. They are active over a wide geographic range, but most severe attack occurs in warmer waters up to 38°N latitude. Isolated severe Limnoria attack sometimes occurs above this latitude. Water-borne CCA and ACA are effective preservatives against Limnoria Tripunctata, Teredo and Bankia.

7 Pholads are usually less damaging than Limnoria and do most damage in warm Gulf Coast, Southern California and Southern Florida waters. Creosote-coal tar is effective against pholads.

8 The retentions are based on two assay zones—0 to 0.50 inch and 0.50 to 2.0 inches.

Water-borne salt preservatives include acid copper chromate (ACC), ammoniacal copper arsenate (ACA), and chromated copper arsenate (CCA). These preservatives leave the wood light green in color, are odorless and paintable. Commercially available timbers such as 4 × 4s and 6 × 6s are usually treated with one of these water-borne salts.

Creosote, one of the earliest wood preservatives, was commonly used on telephone poles and railroad ties. It leaves wood dark brown in color with an oily surface and a strong odor. It is not paintable, highly toxic to plants and marine organisms, and can burn skin upon contact.

Pentachlorophenol in gas is clearly the best treatment for building poles where a natural color is desired. Both this treatment and water-borne salts are equally suitable for poles that will be painted. Creosote, because of its finish and odor, should be avoided where possible.

All of these wood preservatives are highly toxic and are currently on the Environmental Protection Agency's list for review as possible carcinogens. Whenever you work with pressure-treated wood observe the following precautions to minimize the risk of possible contamination.

- Wear gloves and heavy work clothes when handling treated lumber.
- Wear a particle mask and goggles when sawing or sanding.
- Wash your hands before eating or drinking.
- Never burn pressure-treated lumber scraps.

Pressure-treated Timbers

Pressure-treated timbers are available at most lumberyards and building supply outlets. Standard sizes include 4 × 4, 6 × 6, and 8 × 8 timbers that range from 8 to 16 feet long. These timbers are usually southern yellow pine treated with a water-borne salt preservative that turns them light green in color.

Pressure-treated timbers can only be used for buildings where the roof line is 12 feet or less off the ground since 16 feet is the longest standard timber length and at least 4 feet of the timber must be buried in the ground for stability. For small sheds or barns, however, using 6 × 6 or 8 × 8 timbers makes a lot of sense. They are about the same price per foot as pressure-treated poles, the lumberyard can deliver them to the building site, and you can buy the exact size you need.

The other big advantage of building with pressure-treated timbers is that they are planed true on 4 sides. Thus they are easier to plumb to get vertical corners and walls, something that is often hard to do with the best of poles. It is also easier to attach the framing members to timbers since they don't taper or have an irregular surface.

Make sure, when you buy timbers, that they are in fact pressure-treated and not merely surface-dipped in a preservative. Often timbers are sold for landscaping and retaining walls that are

This horse barn was built using pressure-treated 4×4's and 6×6's that are available from any building supply company.

only dipped in preservative. They look the same on the outside, but on the inside the preservative has penetrated only ½-inch or less which is not adequate protection for wood that will be in contact with earth. Pressure-treated timbers always carry a tag or stamp that indicates they were pressure-treated in accordance with AWPA standards and are suitable for prolonged contact with soil.

Cutting Your Own Poles

If pressure-treated poles or timbers are not available or it is not practical to get them to a remote site, you can cut your own poles. Cedar and cyprus are two species of trees that are widely available and make excellent foundation poles. Both have a natural fungicide in their fibers that resists decay. However, don't expect an untreated pole, despite this natural resistance, to last any more than 10 to 15 years unless you are building in a very dry environment.

Untreated poles are often a good choice for livestock housing where low cost and absence of toxic preservatives are the primary considerations rather than permanence. This more than compensates for their relatively short life compared to pressure-treated poles.

This barn is being built with locally cut cedar poles, green lumber, and recycled metal roofing to keep material costs at a minimum.

Do-it-yourself preservative treatments for poles are not recommended for several important reasons.

- Preservatives are highly toxic to humans and animals. Inevitably, when they are used without the proper equipment, there are spills, skin contact, and excessive vapor inhalation.
- Surface painting or dipping is not effective for wood that is in constant contact with the soil, since the preservative cannot penetrate deeply enough.
- It is very likely that the Environmental Protection Agency will soon restrict the use of penta and other preservatives to licensed applicators only, because of the health hazards of improper use.

Framing Lumber

Pole buildings are framed using conventional 2-inch dimensioned lumber for girts, joists, studs, and rafters. The size of the framing members range from 2 × 4s for interior wall studs to double or triple 2 × 12s which span between the poles and carry the entire weight of the floors (see table 3–3). Dimensioned framing lumber is available either planed on 4 sides and kiln-dried or as green, rough-cut lumber from local sawmills.

Kiln-Dried Lumber

Kiln-dried lumber is available from lumberyards and building supply companies in lengths from 8 to 16 feet. It is normally spruce or hemlock that has been dried in ovens to remove moisture and then planed to exact finish dimensions. For example, a 2 × 6 is actually 1½″ × 5½″ after it has been dried and finished. Table 3–4 shows the actual vs. the nominal dimensions of kiln-dried lumber.

Table 3–3

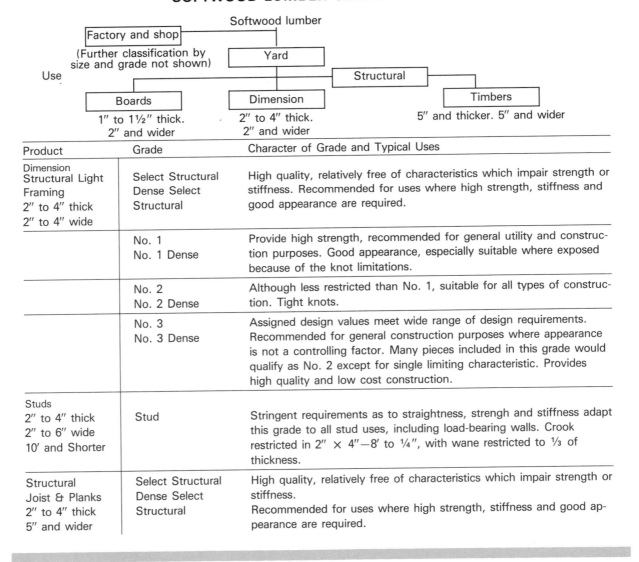

SOFTWOOD LUMBER CLASSIFICATION

Product	Grade	Character of Grade and Typical Uses
Dimension Structural Light Framing 2″ to 4″ thick 2″ to 4″ wide	Select Structural Dense Select Structural	High quality, relatively free of characteristics which impair strength or stiffness. Recommended for uses where high strength, stiffness and good appearance are required.
	No. 1 No. 1 Dense	Provide high strength, recommended for general utility and construction purposes. Good appearance, especially suitable where exposed because of the knot limitations.
	No. 2 No. 2 Dense	Although less restricted than No. 1, suitable for all types of construction. Tight knots.
	No. 3 No. 3 Dense	Assigned design values meet wide range of design requirements. Recommended for general construction purposes where appearance is not a controlling factor. Many pieces included in this grade would qualify as No. 2 except for single limiting characteristic. Provides high quality and low cost construction.
Studs 2″ to 4″ thick 2″ to 6″ wide 10′ and Shorter	Stud	Stringent requirements as to straightness, strength and stiffness adapt this grade to all stud uses, including load-bearing walls. Crook restricted in 2″ × 4″—8′ to ¼″, with wane restricted to ⅓ of thickness.
Structural Joist & Planks 2″ to 4″ thick 5″ and wider	Select Structural Dense Select Structural	High quality, relatively free of characteristics which impair strength or stiffness. Recommended for uses where high strength, stiffness and good appearance are required.

Table 3-3 continued

Product	Grade	Character of Grade and Typical Uses
	No. 1 No. 1 Dense	Provide high strength, recommended for general utility and construction purposes. Good appearance, especially suitable where exposed because of the knot limitations.
	No. 2 No. 2 Dense	Although less restricted than No. 1, suitable for all types of construction. Tight knots.
	No. 3 No. 3 Dense	Assigned stress values meet wide range of design requirements. Recommended for general construction purposes where appearance is not a controlling factor. Many pieces included in this grade would qualify as No. 2 except for single limiting characteristic. Provides high quality and low cost construction.
Light Framing 2" to 4" thick 2" to 4" wide	Construction	Recommended for general framing purposes. Good appearance, strong and serviceable.
	Standard	Recommended for same uses as Construction grade, but allows larger defects.
	Utility	Recommended where combination of strength and economy is desired. Excellent for blocking, plates and bracing.
	Economy	Usable lengths suitable for bracing, blocking, bulkheading and other utility purposes where strength and appearance not controlling factors.

(Product and grade information courtesy Southern Forest Products Association) From: Residential Construction Handbook, Reston Publishing.

Graded lumber. Kiln-dried yard lumber is also graded for its structural characteristics. Knots, checks, and other defects in the grain of lumber can dramatically reduce its ability to carry loads. For example, southern pine that is graded *select structural* is capable of withstanding a bending load of 2,880 pounds whereas *utility* grade southern pine is only rated at 340 pounds. That's almost a ten-fold difference in strength! Table 3–5 lists the bending strengths of Douglas Fir lumber for various grades. Most lumber yards sell *construction* or No. 2 grade lumber, which is what most girt, joist, and rafter tables are based on. Some discount yards, however, will sell utility grade as a special low price sale item. Beware! It's not worth the savings as you'll realize after reviewing the stress tables.

Green Lumber

As an alternative to buying kiln-dried lumber, green or un-dried rough-cut lumber is often available from local sawmills. These are the 2 × 4s and larger stock before they are sent to be kiln-dried and planed. They are wet, heavy, and of slightly differing dimensions. They are also considerably cheaper than their kiln-dried counterparts. Typically, green lumber is 30 percent less expensive than kiln-dried lumber and that can mean substantial savings for the owner-builder whose largest expense is materials.

Table 3-4

NOMINAL AND MINIMUM-DRESSED SIZES OF BOARDS, DIMENSION, AND TIMBERS
(The thicknesses apply to all widths and all widths to all thicknesses.)

		Thicknesses			Face widths	
		Minimum dressed			Minimum dressed	
Item	Nominal	Dry	Green	Nominal	Dry	Green
		Inches	Inches		Inches	Inches
Boards -------------	1	3/4	25/32	2	1-1/2	1-9/16
	1-1/4	1	1-1/32	3	2-1/2	2-9/16
	1-1/2	1-1/4	1-9/32	4	3-1/2	3-9/16
				5	4-1/2	4-5/8
				6	5-1/2	5-5/8
				7	6-1/2	6-5/8
				8	7-1/4	7-1/2
				9	8-1/4	8-1/2
				10	9-1/4	9-1/2
				11	10-1/4	10-1/2
				12	11-1/4	11-1/2
				14	13-1/4	13-1/2
				16	15-1/4	15-1/2
Dimension----------	2	1-1/2	1-9/16	2	1-1/2	1-9/16
	2-1/2	2	2-1/16	3	2-1/2	2-9/16
	3	2-1/2	2-9/16	4	3-1/2	3-9/16
	3-1/2	3	3-1/16	5	4-1/2	4-5/8
				6	5-1/2	5-5/8
				8	7-1/4	7-1/2
				10	9-1/4	9-1/2
				12	11-1/4	11-1/2
				14	13-1/4	13-1/2
				16	15-1/4	15-1/2
Dimension----------	4	3-1/2	3-9/16	2	1-1/2	1-9/16
	4-1/2	4	4-1/16	3	2-1/2	2-9/16
				4	3-1/2	3-9/16
				5	4-1/2	4-5/8
				6	5-1/2	5-5/8
				8	7-1/4	7-1/2
				10	9-1/4	9-1/2
				12	11-1/4	11-1/2
				14	-------	13-1/2
				16	-------	15-1/2
Timbers -------------	5 and thicker	------	1/2 off	8 and Wider	-------	1/2 off

(From: "Wood Structural Design Data," National Forest Products Association.)

Despite its lower cost, green lumber does have some disadvantages.

- As it dries, boards and timbers can warp and split.
- You will probably have to haul it from the sawmill yourself, which will require a large truck.
- If it is not used right away, it will have to be stacked properly with stickers separating each layer so that it will dry without warping and splitting.
- Because of the slightly uneven dimensions of rough-sawn lumber, extra care must be taken when using it for wall and floor framing (see chapter 6).

Rough-sawn green lumber is an excellent and inexpensive siding material. For traditional board and batten siding that is perfect for barns, cabins, as well as finished houses, 1×8 boards can be used. Green board and batten siding can be installed for one-third

Table 3-5

LUMBER GRADES AND STRENGTH

Species and Grade	Size	Normal Duration	Design Value in Bending "F_b"* Snow Loading	7-Day Loading	Modulus of Elasticity "E"	Grading Rules
Douglas Fir—Larch (Surfaced dry or surfaced green)						
Dense Select Structural		2800	3220	3500	1,900,000	
Select Structural		2400	2760	3000	1,800,000	
Dense No. 1		2400	2760	3000	1,900,000	
No. 1 & Appearance		2050	2360	2560	1,800,000	
	2×4					
Dense No. 2		1950	2240	2440	1,700,000	
No. 2		1650	1900	2060	1,700,000	Western Wood
No. 3		925	1060	1160	1,500,000	Products
Stud		925	1060	1160	1,500,000	Association
Construction		1200	1380	1500	1,500,000	
Standard	2×4	675	780	840	1,500,000	
Utility		325	370	410	1,500,000	West Coast
Dense Select Structural		2400	2760	3000	1,900,000	Lumber
Select Structural		2050	2360	2560	1,800,000	Inspection
Dense No. 1	2×5	2050	2360	2560	1,900,000	Bureau
No. 1 & Appearance	and wider	1750	2010	2190	1,800,000	
Dense No. 2		1700	1960	2120	1,700,000	
No. 2		1450	1670	1810	1,700,000	
No. 3		850	980	1060	1,500,000	
Stud		850	980	1060	1,500,000	

(From: "Design Values for Joists," National Forest Products Association.)

*These "F_b" values are for use where repetitive members are spaced not more than 24 inches. For wider spacing, the "F_b" values should be reduced 13 percent.

Values for surfaced dry or surfaced green lumber apply at 19 percent maximum moisture content in use.

the cost of clapboards, and one-half the cost of textured plywood sidings.

Getting It Green

Given the cost-savings associated with using green lumber, it makes sense to check and see if there is a sawmill near you that

Selecting and Storing Green Lumber

When you visit a sawmill to inquire about buying green lumber, you will want to investigate both the price and the quality of lumber that the mill turns out.

Lumber is sold by the board foot. One board foot is the volume of a piece of wood that measures $12 \times 12 \times 1$ inches or 144 cubic inches. The easiest way to figure board feet is to multiply the nominal dimensions together, divide by 12, and then multiply by the length of the piece. Thus a 2×6 is 2 inches times 6 inches divided by 12, or 1 times 8 feet in length, or 8 board feet. A 12-foot 2×4 is 2 times 4 divided by 12, or 8/12 times 12 feet, or again 8 board feet.

To determine the quality of the lumber, first check its nominal dimensions. Because it is rough-cut wood that has not been planed yet, its dimensions will vary over and under the nominal dimensions. Thus one 2×6 may be 5¾ inches and another 6⅛ inches. The best sawmills can hold their tolerances to within ⅛-inch of the nominal size. Be wary of buying lumber that varies more than ¼-inch over or under its nominal size because it will make framing difficult, since there could be as much as ½-inch difference between adjacent pieces.

Also check the lumber for knots and other defects. A piece of wood that is full of knots has much less strength than a piece of clear lumber. The best way to judge lumber is to compare it to the construction grade lumber you get at a local lumberyard. Is it comparable in clearness and straightness of grain? If it looks decidedly more knotty, you may not want to use it for floor girts, joists, and rafters that must have good strength to resist bending. Because the lumber at sawmills has not been graded, what you will find is that in every batch of wood there will be some defective lumber but also some very high quality lumber. Set the less desireable lumber aside for studs or blocking, and use the best for girts and joists.

Green lumber is often 50 percent moisture by weight when it is freshly cut. Thus a green 8-foot 2×6 could contain over 10 pounds of water! It is very important to stack green lumber correctly to facilitate drying, if it is not going to be used immediately. Lumber should be stacked in piles with each layer separated by 1-inch wood *stickers* that allow air flow through the pile. Stacking the lumber in this way also minimizes the twisting, warping, and checking that occur as unrestrained lumber dries. The pile should be covered on top to shed rain, and weighted with cement blocks or rocks to keep the top boards from twisting.

would be willing to supply the lumber for your building project. The first step is to check the Yellow Pages, which will list the larger mills in the area. Oftentimes, however, it is the unlisted small mills that are willing to sell at retail to individuals, and these might not even have a phone. So ask builders in your area if they know of any, and go out and pay these mills a visit to look over their lumber and prices.

Another source of green lumber is small farm or home mills that cut occasionally in their own woodlots. For owner-bulders who own forested land that must be cleared before building, you can often find an operator of a portable mill who can mill your trees into dimensioned lumber right on site.

A final option for builders who have a large tract of forest is to buy your own portable mill or a smaller chain saw mill and do it yourself. Even the smallest saw mill equipment is expensive, and unless you expect to be cutting lumber fairly regularly for your own use or for sale, such a purchase could turn out to be an expensive investment.

Green lumber should always be stacked in a stickered pile to facilitate air drying and minimize warping.

CALCULATING BUILDING LOADS

CHAPTER FOUR

In pole buildings the weight of floors, walls, and the roof is carried by individual poles and the girts that span them. This is a much more efficient and cost-effective method when compared to conventional stud framing, but it requires that the poles, girts, and joists be engineered to carry their respective loads.

This does not mean you must be an engineer to design and build a pole building, but you should understand how loads are distributed in a pole structure, and how to size framing members accordingly. This chapter presents the fundamentals of building load calculation, so anyone who can add and multiply can safely build a pole structure ranging from a 12×12 barn to a two-story house.

It should be noted that the method presented here is highly simplified though accurate enough for designing conventional pole structures. If you are undertaking a complex building that involves unusual shapes and bearing loads, you'll need to consult a building engineer who can help you get the maximum strength with the minimum number of poles and framing.

Selecting Design Loads

The first step in calculating building loads is to make a dimensioned sketch of your building showing the spacing of the poles, location of the carrying girts, and the layout of the floors, walls, and roof. This is very useful in visualizing how all these elements are tied together and supported. Figure 4–1 shows such a sketch of the 24×24 pole cabin that is presented in Part 2 of this book. We will use this cabin as an example for calculating building loads.

Assigning loads. Table 4–1 presents standard design loads (in pounds per square foot) for different parts of a building. We can use this table to assign a maximum or design load to the floors, walls, and roof of the cabin. Notice that there are two different kinds of loads, live and dead. *Live loads* are those associated with people, furniture, snow, or any other load that can come and go periodically. *Dead loads* are those associated with the framing and structure of a building, such as the weight of floor joists, the subfloor, and finished flooring.

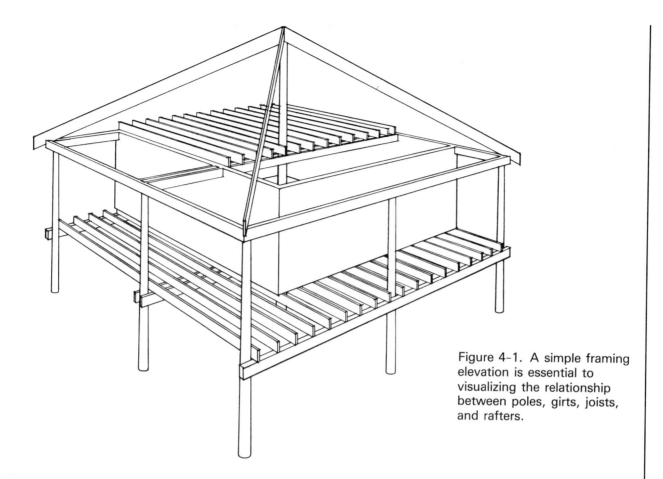

Figure 4-1. A simple framing elevation is essential to visualizing the relationship between poles, girts, joists, and rafters.

Table 4-1

BUILDING DESIGN LOADS

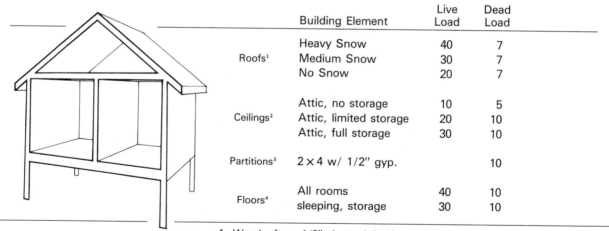

Building Element		Live Load	Dead Load
Roofs[1]	Heavy Snow	40	7
	Medium Snow	30	7
	No Snow	20	7
Ceilings[2]	Attic, no storage	10	5
	Attic, limited storage	20	10
	Attic, full storage	30	10
Partitions[3]	2 × 4 w/ 1/2″ gyp.		10
Floors[4]	All rooms	40	10
	sleeping, storage	30	10

1. Wood rafters, 1/2″ plywood decking, shingle or metal roofing. For slate, tile, or heavy roofing add 10 lbs. to dead load.
2. Wood joist and 1/2″ gypsum ceiling. Wood subfloor for attic w/ storage.
3. 2 × 4 studs, 16″ o.c. w/ 1/2″ gypsum both sides.
4. Wood joists, 3/4″ ply. subfloor and finish floor. For ceramic tile add 10 lbs. to dead load.

The values given in Table 4–1 cover most situations found in residential building, but you should always check local building codes to see what values they specify for design loading. For instance, you may live in a low snow area that would normally call for rafter framing that supports a 20 lb. live load, yet the local codes may call for a 40 lb. live load framing due to a freak snowstorm five years ago that collapsed many roofs in the area. Appendix E shows snow loads for different parts of the United States that will serve as a guide for choosing the correct live load factor for your particular building site. Appendix G lists weights for agricultural products that will help you determine live loads for barns or other non-residential structures.

Using Table 4–1 we can assign the proper design loads to our pole cabin's floors, walls, and roof. The first floor should be designed to carry the conventional 40 lbs. per sq. ft. live load and a dead load of 10 lbs. per sq. ft. for the framing, or a total of 50 lbs. per sq. ft. The walls have a dead weight of 10 lbs. per sq. ft. The loft, since it is used only for sleeping and light storage, can be designed to carry a 20 lb. per sq. ft. live load and a 10 lb. per sq. ft. dead load, or 30 lbs. per sq. ft. The roof, since we will be building

Why Poles are so Strong

Shipbuilders have traditionally used poles made from large straight trees for the masts of sailing ships. They were careful to remove as little wood as possible aside from the outer bark, because they knew it would dramatically weaken the mast if they carved off too many of the outer fibers. Early engineers often scoffed at this as mere shipbuilding superstition because they felt that wood was wood, whether it was in the shape of a tree or a hewn beam of the same size.

Modern research, however, has shown that the shipbuilders were right; a tree is something more than just a stick of wood. In fact, a tree can have up to twice the bending strength of a dimensioned piece of lumber of the same size. The way the tree accomplishes this is by "prestressing" its fibers as it grows. The outer wood of a tree is normally in tension (reportedly at an amazing 2,000 p.s.i.) and the inner wood is in compression. Since wood is much weaker in compression than in tension, this outer tension counteracts the potentially disasterous effect of the wind compressing the wood fibers as it bends it. Because of the outer tension, the tree must be bent considerably before it even goes into compression. This same technique is used with modern concrete structures to strengthen them against breaking under tension.

Pole building thus takes advantage of nature's remarkable engineering by using poles that retain much of the original shape of the trees they came from. While modern engineering has produced many new and very strong building materials, it still hasn't come close to matching the strength of a tree, pound for pound, dollar for dollar.

in a moderate snow area should carry 30 lbs. per sq. ft. live load and a 7 lb. per sq. ft. dead load.

We can now multiply these design loads by the square footage involved to get the total maximum weight of the building elements. The first floor is 24 × 24 or 576 sq. ft. Multiplied by 50 lbs. per sq. ft. we get a total load of 28,800 lbs. In a similar manner we can calculate the weight of the individual walls, the loft area, and the roof (see figure 4–2). Notice that the area of the roof is calculated using its horizontal projection, not actual sloped area. The horizontal projection is used for all sloped surfaces since the force of gravity and hence the loading weight is vertical not perpendicular to the roof surface.

Figure 4-2. Design loading on pole cabin.

POLE CABIN LOADS

1. First Floor:
Area = 24 ft. by 24 ft. = 576 sq. ft.
Live Load = 40 lbs./sq. ft. = 576 sq. ft. × 40 lbs./sq. ft. = 23,040 lbs.
Dead Load = 10 lbs./sq. ft. = 576 sq. ft. × 10 lbs./sq. ft. = 5,760 lbs.
Total Load = 50 lbs./sq. ft. = 576 sq. ft. × 50 lbs./sq. ft. = 28,800 lbs.

2. Loft Floor:
Area = 12 ft. by 18 ft. = 216 sq. ft.
Live Load = 20 lbs./sq. ft. = 216 sq. ft. × 20 lbs./sq. ft. = 4,320 lbs.
Dead Load = 10 lbs./sq. ft. = 216 sq. ft. × 10 lbs./sq. ft. = 2,160 lbs.
Total Load = 30 lbs./sq. ft. = 216 sq. ft. × 30 lbs./sq. ft. = 6,480 lbs.

3. South and West Walls:
Area of each wall = 19 ft. by 10 ft. = 190 sq. ft.
Dead load = 10 lbs./sq. ft. = 190 sq. ft. × 10 lbs./sq. ft. = 1,900 lbs.

4. North and East Walls:
Area of each wall = 19 ft. by 8 ft. = 152 sq. ft.
Dead Load = 10 lbs./sq. ft. = 152 sq. ft. × 10 lbs./sq. ft. = 1,520 lbs.

5. Roof:
Area = 25 ft. by 25 ft. (horizontal projection) = 625 sq. ft.
Live Load = 30 lbs./sq. ft. = 625 sq. ft. × 30 lbs./sq. ft. = 18,750 lbs.
Dead Load = 7 lbs./sq. ft. = 625 sq. ft. × 7 lbs./sq. ft. = 4,375 lbs.
Total Load = 37 lbs./sq. ft. = 625 sq. ft. × 37 lbs./sq. ft. = 23,125 lbs.

Uniform Loading on Poles and Girts

We now know how much weight each element of the building's frame will be carrying when it is fully loaded. But that does not tell us how this load is being carried by the poles and girts, and that is what we are really interested in. Once we know how much weight individual poles and girts are carrying, we can then size them correctly to carry the load.

For our simple analysis of building loads we will assume that all loads are carried uniformly across a support such as a girt, joist, or rafter. This will almost always be true of floors and roofs, but care should be taken when designing for point loads. A *point load* is an object such as a hot water tank that might weigh up to 1000 pounds when full and be placed on a few square feet of floor area. Obviously, a 1000 pound tank resting on only 2 floor joists is not the same as 1000 pounds evenly distributed across a 12 × 12 floor. Special care must be taken to identify any point loads and to strengthen the framing at that point accordingly.

Load distribution. Assuming uniform loading, we can see how girts and poles act together to support a pole structure. Figure 4–3 shows how loading is distributed on a beam (such as a girt) supported by differing numbers of columns (such as poles). When a girt is supported evenly between two end poles, the weight is evenly distributed between both poles. But what happens when you add a center pole? Do all three poles carry one-third of the weight? The answer is no because each span must carry half the weight of the entire beam; therefore, the outside pole carries half of this or one-quarter of the load. This leaves the middle pole carrying ¼ plus ¼ or ½ of the load. As you can see from figure 4–3, an easy rule of thumb is that the interior poles or columns support the load divided by the number of spans, and the two end poles support one-half this much.

Calculating Pole Loading

We can now use this information on design loads and beam loading to calculate the loads on individual poles. It is simply a matter of assigning part of the weight of each framing element to individual poles.

Continuing with our pole cabin as the example, we can see that the first floor and walls are supported by three rows of poles and the girts that span them. There is the south row, middle row, and north row. The loft is supported only by the middle row and the north row. The roof is equally supported by four sets of girts: south, east, west, and north.

First, we'll determine the load on the entire south row of poles and then break that into loads on individual poles. As summarized in figure 4–4, the south row of poles supports one-quarter the weight of the first floor because it is uniformly distributed across the three supporting rows of poles. One-half of the south wall is carried by the poles because its weight is equally distributed between the south and middle rows. Only one-third of the east and west walls bears on the floor between the south and middle poles, and therefore their contribution to the south poles is ⅓ times ½, or ⅙ of their weight. Finally, the south poles carry one-fourth of the roof load.

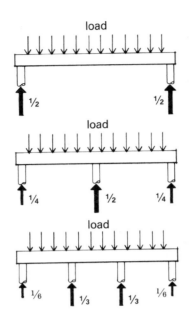

Figure 4–3. Uniform loading on a beam and supporting columns.

CABIN POLE LOADING

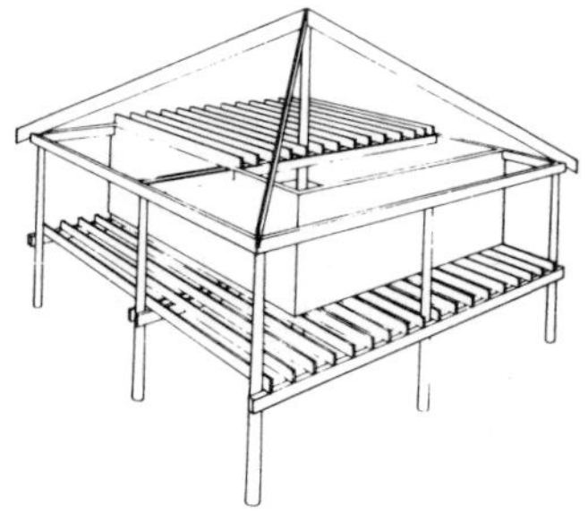

1. Loading on South Row of Poles:

¼ of first floor	=	28,800 lbs. ÷ 4	=	7,200 lbs.
½ of south wall	=	1,900 lbs. ÷ 2	=	950 lbs.
½ of ⅓ of west wall	=	1,900 lbs. ÷ 2 ÷ 3	=	316 lbs.
½ of ⅓ of east wall	=	1,520 lbs. ÷ 2 ÷ 3	=	253 lbs.
¼ of roof	=	23,125 lbs. ÷ 4	=	5,781 lbs.

Total Load on Row	=	14,500 lbs.
Middle pole carries ½ of load	=	7,250 lbs.
Each outside pole carries ¼ of load	=	3,800 lbs.
plus ¼ load of E. and W. roof section	=	1,445 lbs.
Total load on each outside pole	=	5,245 lbs.

2. Loading on Middle Row of Poles:

½ of first floor	=	28,800 lbs. ÷ 2	=	14,400 lbs.
½ of south wall	=	1,900 lbs. ÷ 2	=	950 lbs.
½ of west wall	=	1,900 lbs. ÷ 2	=	950 lbs.
½ of east wall	=	1,520 lbs. ÷ 2	=	760 lbs.
½ of loft	=	6,480 lbs. ÷ 2	=	3,240 lbs.

Total Load on Row	=	20,300 lbs.
Middle pole carries ½ of load	=	10,150 lbs.
Each outside pole carries ¼ of load	=	5,075 lbs.
plus ½ load of E. and W. roof sections	=	2,890 lbs.
Total load on each outside pole	=	7,965 lbs.

3. Loading on North Row of Poles:

¼ of first floor	=	28,800 lbs. ÷ 4	=	7,200 lbs.
½ of ⅔ of east wall	=	1,520 lbs. ÷ 3	=	507 lbs.
½ of ⅔ of west wall	=	1,900 lbs. ÷ 3	=	633 lbs.
all of north wall	=	1,520 lbs.	=	1,520 lbs.
½ of loft	=	6,480 lbs. ÷ 2	=	3,240 lbs.
¼ of roof	=	23,125 lbs. ÷ 4	=	5,781 lbs.

Total Load on Row	=	18,881 lbs.
Middle pole carries ½ of load	=	9,440 lbs.
Each outside pole carries ¼ of load	=	4,720 lbs.
plus ¼ load of E. and W. roof sections	=	1,445 lbs.
Total load on each outside pole	=	6,165 lbs.

Figure 4-4. Pole loading on Cabin.

These individual loadings are then added up to give the total loading on the south row of poles. Since there are three poles and we assume uniform loading, that means the middle pole must carry one-half the total weight and the outer poles one-quarter of the weight. However, the outer poles also carry one-quarter of the roof load for the east and west rafter girts, so this additional weight must be added to each outer pole.

Optimum pole loading. We can see that the middle pole of the south row is carrying about 7,150 pounds. This is a good weight for an 6-inch pole, neither too much or too little. The American Wood Preservers Institute (AWPI) recommends 8,000 pounds as a good working load per pole and uses that amount as the basis of their pole embedment charts that are presented in chapter 5. Using poles with less than 8,000 pounds on them increases the cost and decreases the efficiency of pole building, while using poles with twice the load requires careful engineering and embedment. In general, poles should be spaced to carry about 6,000 to 12,000 pounds.

The loading on the middle and north rows of poles can be calculated in the same manner. Figure 4–4 summarizes these calculations and shows that the middle pole of the middle row carries the greatest weight, **10,150 lbs.** This is well within our range for pole loading, and thus we can use the standard pole embedment depths and methods as recommended in chapter 5.

Calculating Girt Loading

While it is important to verify that individual pole loading is within our safe range of values, it is much more critical to calculate the loading on girts, so that they are sized correctly. The girts will be made from double or triple 2 × 8s or larger stock, and it is important for safety and economy that they be sized to carry the maximum design load, but not be any larger.

To size the girts we will again add up the weights of the building elements that they support, and then assign these weights to individual spans between the poles. We can then use table 4–2, **Safe Loads For Beams**, to pick the correct size of girt.

Starting with the first floor girts on the south row of poles, we can add up all the elements that they support. They support one-quarter of the first floor weight, one-half the south wall, and $\frac{1}{3}$ times $\frac{1}{2}$ of the east and west wall. This is exactly the same as when we added up the weight on the poles, except we leave the roof out since it is supported by its own set of girts.

The total weight on the south floor girts is 8,718 lbs. Since there are two equal 12-foot sections of girts, each must carry 4,359 lbs. Now looking at table 4–2, under 12-foot spans we see that a 2 × 12 will carry 2,109 lbs. Two 2 × 12 girts would carry twice as much or 4,218 lbs. We could probably use a double 2 × 12 to carry our load even though we are 150 pounds over our "safe" load. If we aren't sure of the quality of our lumber, however, we should play it safe and use a triple 2 × 12 that will more than meet the requirements for our design loads.

In a similar manner, we can figure the loading and appropriate size for all our other girts. Figure 4–5 summarizes these calculations. Notice on the north row of poles, that we have to use triple 2 × 12 girts to support the extra weight of the north wall and loft.

CABIN GIRT LOADING

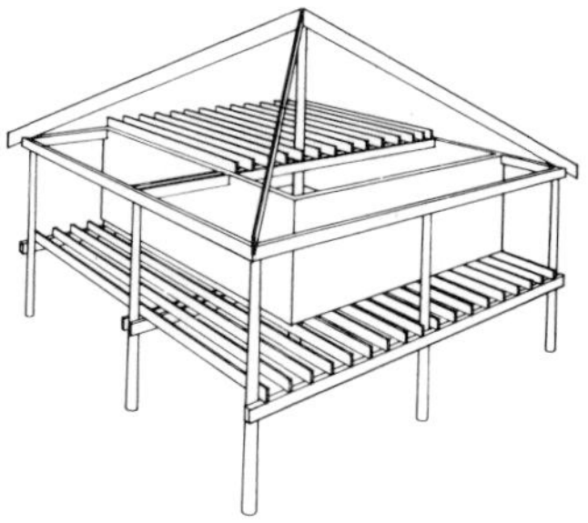

1. South Row Floor Girts:

1/4 of first floor	=	28,800 lbs. ÷ 4	=	7,200 lbs.
½ of south wall	=	1,900 lbs. ÷ 2	=	950 lbs.
½ of ⅓ of west wall	=	1,900 lbs. ÷ 2 ÷ 3	=	316 lbs.
½ of ⅓ of east wall	=	1,520 lbs. ÷ 2 ÷ 3	=	253 lbs.
Total Load on Girts			=	8,719 lbs.

Each 12 ft. section carries one-half the load = 4,359 lbs.
Three 2 × 12's can carry 6,327 lbs. over 12 ft. span

2. Middle Row Floor Girts:

½ of first floor	=	28,800 lbs. ÷ 2	=	14,400 lbs.
½ of south wall	=	1,900 lbs. ÷ 2	=	950 lbs.
½ of west wall	=	1,900 lbs. ÷ 2	=	950 lbs.
½ of east wall	=	1,520 lbs. ÷ 2	=	760 lbs.
Total Load on Girts			=	17,060 lbs.

Each 12 ft. section carries one-half the load = 8,530 lbs.
Two double 2 × 12's can carry 8,436 lbs. over 12 ft. span.

3. North Row Floor Girts:

¼ of first floor	=	28,800 lbs. ÷ 4	=	7,200 lbs.
½ of ⅔ of west wall	=	1,900 lbs. ÷ 3	=	633 lbs.
½ of ⅔ of east wall	=	1,520 lbs. ÷ 3	=	507 lbs.
all of north wall	=	1,520 lbs.	=	1,520 lbs.
Total Load on Girts			=	9,860 lbs.

Each 12 ft. section carries one-half the load = 4,930 lbs.
Three 2 × 12's can carry 6,327 lbs. over 12 ft. span.

4. Loft Floor Girts:

½ loft	=	6,480 lbs. ÷ 2	=	3,240 lbs.

Each 12 ft. section carries one-half the load = 1,620 lbs.
Double 2 × 8 can carry 1,752 lbs. over 12 ft. span

5. S.,E., and W. Rafter Girts:

¼ roof	=	23,125 lbs. ÷ 4	=	5,781 lbs.

Each 12 ft. section carries one-half the load = 2,890 lbs.
Double 2 × 12 can carry 4,218 lbs. over 12 ft. span.

6. North Rafter Girts:

¼ roof	=	23,125 lbs. ÷ 4	=	5,781 lbs.
½ loft	=	6,480 lbs. ÷ 2	=	3,240 lbs.
Total Load on Girts			=	9,021 lbs.

Each 12 ft. section carries one-half the load = 4,510 lbs.
Three 2 × 12's can carry 6,327 lbs. over 12 ft. span.

Figure 4–5. Girt loading on Cabin.

Table 4-2

SAFE LOAD FOR BEAMS

Nominal Size	Distance of Span							
	6'	8'	10'	12'	14'	16'	18'	20'
2 × 4	408	306						
2 × 6	1008	756	605	504				
2 × 8	1752	1314	1051	876	750	657	584	
2 × 10	2852	2139	1711	1426	1222	1069	950	855
2 × 12	4218	3164	2531	2109	1808	1582	1406	1265
4 × 4	952	714	571					
6 × 6	3697	2772	2218	1848	1584	1386	1232	1109
8 × 8		7031	5625	4687	4017	3515	3125	2812
10 × 10		14289	11431	9526	8165	7144	6350	5715
12 × 12		25347	20278	16898	14484	12673	11265	10139

(Adapted from: "Wood Structural Design Data," National Forest Products Association.)

Note: All loads in pounds, uniformly loaded across span.
Wood fiber bending stress (Fb) = 1200 lbs.
All calculations based on finished (S4) dimensioned lumber.

Safe ranges. If you are wondering if we're cutting our safety margin a little thin using two double 2 × 12s as middle girts, remember that table 4-2 lists *safe* loads for beams to carry. This means that the girt can safely and continuously carry our 40 lb. per sq. ft. live load and 10 lb. per sq. ft. dead load — the equivalent of 150 people in our cabin, if we could get them all in. It is very seldom that a structure has to stand up to a design load, but for safety we want to make sure it can. Our double 2 × 12s are about 1 percent under our safe load and is therefore acceptable.

Also, in actuality, a double 2 × 12 that is well-spiked together has slightly more than double the loadbearing strength of a single 2 × 12. But because double girts are often placed independently of each other on opposite sides of the poles, to be conservative, you should assume a double girt has only double the carrying capacity of a single girt of equivalent size.

It should also be noted that table 4-2 is based on good quality, construction grade lumber that is dry. Green lumber, because of its moisture content, can have 25 percent less strength. But it also has larger dimensions than commercial kiln-dried lumber which offsets this effect. When the green lumber has dried, of course, it will be stronger than commercial kiln-dried stock, but that may take six months to a year of air drying.

In general, you will want to meet or exceed the requirements for safe loads on girts. This is especially true if you are not using high quality, kiln-dried lumber. When using green lumber, you can still use the safe loading tables because even though green lumber is 25 percent weaker than kiln-dried lumber due to its moisture, it is 50 percent stronger because of its larger dimensions.

Sizing Joists and Rafters

Now that we know our pole spacing and girt size, we can calculate what size of floor joists and rafters to use. You are probably wondering whether we have to add up all the building weights again. The answer, thank goodness, is no. All we have to do is look up the correct size in table 4–3.

Table 4–3 lists the maximum span of joists and rafters for various loadings and spacings. There are six categories of load situations. Column 3, for example, is for floor joists that support sleeping areas or attic storage that are rated at 30 lbs. live load and 10 lbs. dead load. Column 6 is for rafters with a slope greater than 3 in 12 with a 40 lb. live load and 7 lb. dead load. By selecting the

Table 4–3

JOISTS AND RAFTER SPANS

Size	Spacing	#1.	#2.	#3.	#4.	#5.	#6.
2 × 4	12″	11-3	8-11			9-6	7-3
	16″	10-3	8-1			8-3	6-3
	24″	8-11	7-1			6-9	5-1
2 × 6	12″	17-8	14-1	10-9	9-9	15-0	11-4
	16″	16-1	12-9	9-9	8-10	13-0	9-10
	24″	14-1	11-2	8-6	7-9	10-7	8-0
2 × 8	12″	23-4	18-6	14-2	12-10	19-9	14-11
	16″	21-2	16-10	12-10	11-8	17-1	12-11
	24″	18-6	14-8	11-3	10-2	13-11	10-7
2 × 10	12″	29-9	23-8	18-0	16-5	25-2	19-1
	16″	27-1	21-6	16-5	14-11	21-10	16-6
	24″	23-8	18-9	14-4	13-0	17-10	13-6
2 × 12	12″			21-11	19-11		
	16″			19-11	18-1		
	24″			17-5	15-10		

(Adapted from: "Span Tables for Joists and Rafters," National Forest Products Association.)

#1. Ceiling Joists: No attic storage, drywall ceiling.
   Live load = 10 lbs/sq.ft. Dead load = 5 lbs/sq. ft.
#2. Ceiling Joists: Attic storage, drywall ceiling.
   Live load = 20 lbs/sq.ft. Dead load = 10 lbs/sq. ft.
#3. Floor Joists: Sleeping areas or attic storage.
   Live load = 30 lbs/sq.ft. Dead load = 10 lbs/sq. ft.
#4. Floor Joists: All areas.
   Live load = 40 lbs/sq.ft. Dead load = 10 lbs/sq. ft.
#5. Rafters: Greater than 3 in 12 slope, low wind and snow loading.
   Live load = 20 lbs/sq.ft. Dead load = 7 lbs/sq. ft.
#6. Rafters: Greater than 3 in 12 slope, high wind and snow loading.
   Live load = 40 lbs/sq.ft. Dead load = 7 lbs/sq. ft.

Note: All rafter spans measured along horizontal roof projection
   Maximum fiber bending stress (Fb) = 1200 lbs
   Maximum modulus of elasticity (E) = 1,200,000 psi

column appropriate to your use, you can look up the safe span for different size lumber placed at either 12, 16, or 24-inch spacing.

Our floor joists for our pole cabin would fall under column 4. In that column, we can see that 2 × 8 joists placed 16 inches on center (o.c.) can have a clear span of 11 ft. 8 inches (11–8). This is exactly our span between the outside and middle girts. We could also select to use 2 × 10 joists 24 inches on center (o.c.), which will span 13 ft. 0 inches (13–0). The choice would depend on what type of subflooring and flooring we plan to use.

Table 4–3 lists spans for joists and rafters that coincide with the vast majority of building situations. If you need to find safe spans for joists that must carry an 80 lb. live load, for heavy equipment for example, consult a wood construction handbook. *Wood Structural Design Data* is one such manual that lists beam spans, joist and rafter spans, as well as other useful data. See the bibliography in appendix A for further references.

POLE FOUNDATIONS

Because poles serve as framing members as well as a foundation in pole construction, it is critical that they be sized and installed properly. Poles support the weight of a building as in a conventional foundation, but they also resist lateral and uplift forces such as winds and possible flooding. A properly embedded pole is like a tree with a large tap root; it is completely self-supporting and can withstand even strong hurricane-force winds.

Pole Selection and Layout

There are no simple methods to determine the exact diameter of pole you should use. There are general rules of thumb, however. For single story buildings, class 6 and 7 poles are used, with tip diameters of 5½ to 4¾ inches, respectively. For taller two-story buildings, class 2 to 5 poles are used, with tip diameters of 8 to 6 inches. For still taller buildings, class 1 and 2 poles are used with tip diameters of 8½ and 8 inches (see table 3–1). Because of the wind loading pressure on tall buildings, it often pays to get professional engineering advice when building higher than two stories.

The layout of the poles will depend on the floor plan of the building and your building loads. Typical pole spacing is often 6, 8, or 10 feet on center (o.c.), which is a modular spacing that allows efficient use of standard framing lumber for girts. As discusssed in chapter 4, figure your building loads on the poles and on the girts. In general, 6,000 to 12,000 pounds per pole is a good range. Greater loads require a more expensive girt system, and lesser loads mean more poles and foundation expense.

After you have calculated the pole spacing, make a scale drawing showing the placement of all the foundation poles and how the girts attach to them. This will help you visualize the construction process and ensure that your pole and girt arrangement will in fact go together.

Excavation Layout

The first step is to lay out the building lines and batter boards. *Building lines*, marked by a taut string, make it easy to precisely lo-

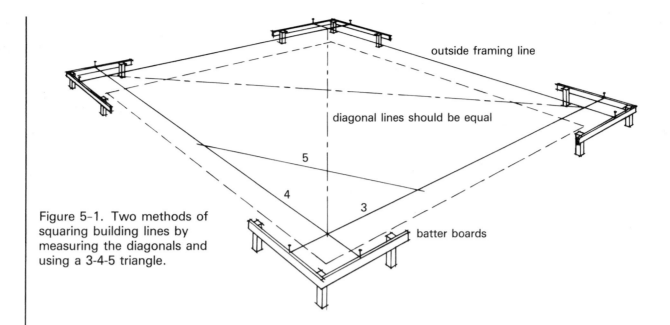

outside framing line

diagonal lines should be equal

5

4

3

batter boards

Figure 5-1. Two methods of squaring building lines by measuring the diagonals and using a 3-4-5 triangle.

cate the foundation holes, the outside of the pole frame, and the corners. *Batter boards* are used to hold the string in the corners, so the string can be removed during excavation and pole embedment, and then reattached to check the building lines without going through the whole layout process again.

Using a 50-foot tape measure, locate the outer corners of the building and mark them with temporary stakes. The outside of a building should always be measured to the outside of the wall framing, whether it be girts or regular stud framing. The placement of the poles will then be measured from this reference point, either inside or outside of the wall.

The most accurate way to measure if the building lines are square (and you do want them to be exactly square), is to measure the diagonals between corners and adjust them until they are equal. This will work for any type of rectangle or square and give you 90 degree angles in each corner.

Using a 3-4-5 triangle. Another method to check squareness when string lines are in place is to use a 3-4-5 triangle. Any right triangle will have sides that are proportional to 3:4:5. Thus at a corner, you can mark off 3 feet on one leg, 4 feet on the other leg, and adjust the hypotenuse between the two points until it measures exactly 5 feet. The corner now has to be a right angle. This is a useful method to use when you are initially laying out the corners, and should be used in conjunction with measuring the diagonals.

When the corners are marked off, put together a batter board for each corner that has at least 4-foot sides attached to sturdy stakes. Following the diagonal lines out from the corner, set up the batter boards 2 feet out from the corner, so they are out of the way of the excavation. The top of the batter boards all need to be at the same elevation, if possible, so that the strings are level. You can use either a line level or a hose with a water level attachment to do this.

If the batter boards cannot be placed at the same elevation, you will want to use a plumb bob dropped from a level tape measure whenever reading distances.

Rechecking the building line. With the boards in place, attach the strings to the batter boards so they intersect at the corners of the building. Recheck the building lines both for length and squareness, and then mark the string position on the batter board by driving a nail into the top of it. You can now put up and take down the strings whenever you need to without disturbing your building layout.

With the building lines in place, measure to the center of the foundation poles which will be either inside or outside of the lines. Use a plumb bob and a tape to measure from the strings to the center of each pole. Stakes should be driven in the ground to mark the center of each pole.

Figure 5–2, for example, shows a pole layout with the poles outside the framing. The center of the pole has been moved out from the outside of the framing ½-inch for plywood siding, another 1½ inches to allow extra clearance from an irregular pole, and 4 inches for half the pole's bottom diameter, or a total of 6 inches.

When the centers of all the foundation holes have been marked, including any interior pole supports, remove the layout strings and coil them on the batter boards for later use.

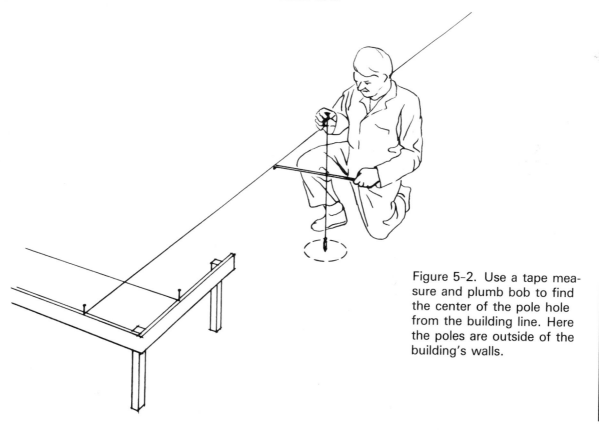

Figure 5–2. Use a tape measure and plumb bob to find the center of the pole hole from the building line. Here the poles are outside of the building's walls.

Calculating Embedment Depth

Pole embedment depth should always be below the frost line, which is the average depth of in-ground frost. A general chart of frost lines for the United States is shown in table 5–1, but more specific information for your locality can be obtained from the National Weather Service. If a pole is not put below the frost line, it can heave in winter and often continue to rise year after year as it is pushed up in winter and earth fills in underneath it.

The depth of pole embedment is a function of the unsupported height of the pole, the pole spacing, and the type of soil. The AWPI has devised a simple method for calculating pole embedment depths as a function of these values. It is presented in tables 5–2 through 5–6.

Table 5–2 presents different soil types, their characteristics and bearing capacity, and their classifications into good, average,

Table 5–1

AVERAGE DEPTH OF FROST PENETRATION (INCHES)

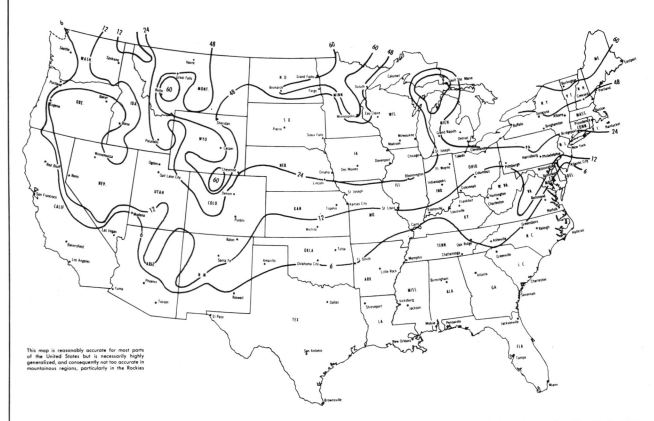

(From: Strock and Koral, Handbook of Air Conditioning, Heating and Ventilating, 2nd Edition. Industrial Press Inc. New York, N.Y.)

or below average for using the AWPI charts. By digging a few test holes, you should be able to classify the soils at your building site fairly easily.

Tables 5–3 through 5–6 present embedment depths as a function of the unsupported height of a pole (H), the pole spacing in feet, the diameter of the bearing surface in inches (D), and the pole's tip diameter. Table 5–3 should be used for pole-framed buildings on slopes of less that 1:10. Table 5–4 is for pole-framed buildings on slopes of up to 1:1. Table 5–5 is for platform-framed buildings on slopes of less than 1:10. Table 5–6 is for platform-framed buildings on slopes up to 1:1.

Table 5-2

SOIL TYPES

AWPI Class	Characteristics	Description
Good	Bearing strength: 6000 PSI Drainage: good Frost heave potential: low	Well-graded sands and gravels Hardpan Graded fine and coarse sands
Average	Bearing strength: 3000 PSI Drainage: medium Frost heave potential: med.	Poorly-graded sands and gravels Silty sand and gravel mixtures Clayey sand and gravel mixtures
Below Average	Bearing strength: 1500 PSI Drainage: poor Frost heave potential: high	Silty or clayey fine sands Inorganic silts Plastic clays

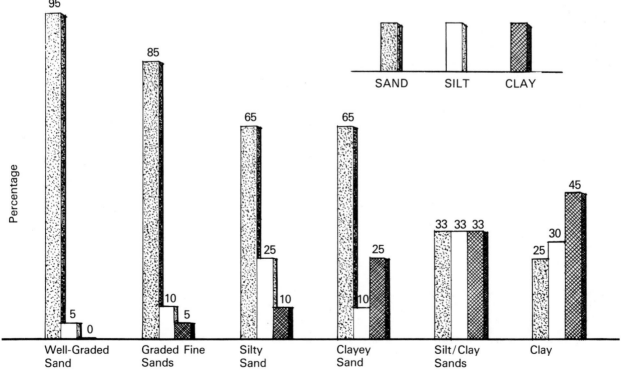

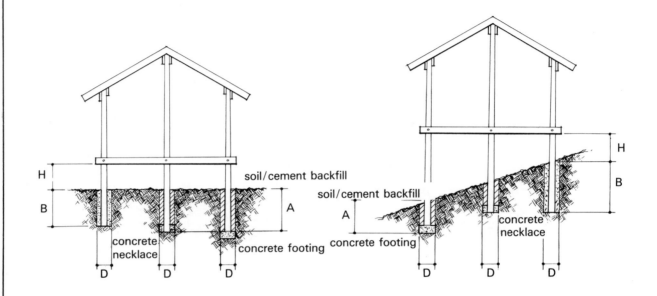

Table 5-3

EMBEDMENT DEPTHS FOR POLES IN POLE-FRAME BUILDINGS ON SITES WITH SLOPES LESS THAN 1:10

H, feet	Pole Spacing, feet	Good Soil Embedment Depth, feet A	B	D, inches	Tip Size, inches	Average Soil Embedment Depth, feet A	B	D, inches	Tip Size, inches	Below Average Soil Embedment Depth, feet A	B	D, inches	Tip Size, inches
	8	5.0	4.0	18	6	6.5	5.0	24	6	•	6.0	36	6
1-1/2 to 3	10	5.5	4.0	21	7	7.0	5.0	30	7	•	6.5	42	7
	12	6.0	4.5	24	7	7.5	5.5	36	7	•	7.0	48	7
	8	6.0	4.0	18	7	7.5	5.5	24	7	•	7.0	36	7
3 to 8	10	6.0	4.5	21	8	8.0	6.0	30	8	•	7.5	42	8
	12	6.5	5.0	24	8	•	6.0	36	8	•	8.0	48	8

(Adapated from: FHA Pole House Construction, AWPI.)

•Embedment depth is greater than eight feet, considered excessively expensive.
Note: Where a concrete floor slab is used at grade, embedment depths may be reduced to 70 percent of those shown.

H = Unsupported height of pole.
A = Embedment depth, using backfill of tamped earth, sand, gravel, or crushed rock.
B = Embedment depth, using backfill of concrete or soil/cement.
D = Bearing diameter.

Table 5–4a

EMBEDMENT DEPTHS FOR LONGER, DOWNHILL POLES OF POLE-FRAME BUILDINGS ON SITES WITH SLOPES UP TO 1:1

Soil Strength	Embedment Depth, feet		
	Slope of Grade		
	Up to 1:3	Up to 1:2	Up to 1:1
Below Average	4.5	6.0	•
Average	4.0	5.0	7.0
Good	4.0	4.0	6.0

(Adapted from: FHA Pole House Construction, AWPI.)

H = Unsupported height of uphill pole.
A = Embedment depth, using backfill of tamped earth, sand, gravel or crushed rock.
B = Embedment depth, using backfill of concrete or soil/cement.
D = Bearing diameter.

Table 5–4b

EMBEDMENT DEPTHS FOR SHORTER, UPHILL POLES IN POLE-FRAME BUILDINGS ON SITES WITH SLOPES UP TO 1:1

H, feet	Pole Spacing, feet	Good Soil				Average Soil				Below Average Soil			
		Embedment Depth, feet		D, inches	Tip Size, inches	Embedment Depth, feet		D, inches	Tip Size, inches	Embedment Depth, feet		D, inches	Tip Size, inches
		A	B			A	B			A	B		
1-1/2 to 3	6	7.0	5.0	18	8	•	6.5	18	8	•	•	•	•
	8	7.5	5.5	18	9	•	7.0	24	9	•	•	•	•
	10	•	6.0	21	9	•	8.0	30	9	•	•	•	•
	12	•	6.5	24	10†	•	•	•	•	•	•	•	•
3 to 8	6	7.5	5.5	18	8	•	7.0	18	8	•	•	•	•
	8	8.0	6.0	18	9	•	8.0	24	9	•	•	•	•
	10	•	7.0	21	10†	•	•	•	•	•	•	•	•
	12	•	7.0	24	11†	•	•	•	•	•	•	•	•

(Adapted from: FHA Pole House Construction, AWPI.)

•Embedment depth is greater than eight feet, considered excessively expensive.
†These tip diameters may be decreased one inch, provided embedment is increased by one-half foot.

Table 5-5

EMBEDMENT DEPTHS FOR POLES IN PLATFORM BUILDINGS ON SITES WITH SLOPES LESS THAN 1:10

H, feet	Pole Spacing, feet	Good Soil Embedment Depth, feet A	B	D, inches	Tip Size, inches	Average Soil Embedment Depth, feet A	B	D, inches	Tip Size, inches	Below Average Soil Embedment Depth, feet A	B	D, inches	Tip Size, inches
1-1/2 to 3	8	4.0	4.0	18	5	5.5	4.0	24	5	7.0	5.0	36	5
	10	4.5	4.0	21	5	6.0	4.0	30	5	8.0	5.5	42	5
	12	5.0	4.0	24	5	6.5	4.5	36	5	•	5.5	48	5
3 to 8	8	5.0	4.0	18	6	6.5	4.5	24	6	•	6.0	36	6
	10	5.5	4.0	21	7	7.0	5.0	30	7	•	6.5	42	7
	12	6.0	4.5	24	7	7.5	5.5	36	7	•	7.0	48	7

(Adapted from: FHA Pole House Construction, AWPI.)

•Embedment depth is greater than eight feet, considered excessively expensive.

H = Unsupported height of pole.
A = Embedment depth, using backfill of tamped earth, sand, gravel, or crushed rock.
B = Embedment depth, using backfill of concrete or soil/cement.
D = Bearing diameter.

Table 5-6

EMBEDMENT DEPTHS FOR SHORTER UPHILL POLES IN PLATFORM BUILDINGS ON SITES WITH SLOPES UP TO 1:1

H, feet	Pole Spacing, feet	Good Soil Embedment Depth, feet A	B	D, inches	Tip Size, inches	Average Soil Embedment Depth, feet A	B	D, inches	Tip Size, inches	Below Average Soil Embedment Depth, feet A	B	D, inches	Tip Size, inches
1-1/2 to 3	6	5.5	4.0	18	6	7.5	5.0	18	6	•	7.0	24	6
	8	6.5	4.5	18	7	•	6.0	24	7	•	8.0	36	7
	10	7.0	5.0	21	7	•	6.5	30	7	•	•	•	•
	12	7.5	5.5	24	8	•	7.0	36	8	•	•	•	•
3 to 8	6	7.0	5.0	18	8	•	6.5	18	8	•	8.0	24	8
	8	7.5	5.5	18	9	•	7.0	24	9	•	•	•	•
	10	•	6.0	21	10†	•	7.5	30	10†	•	•	•	•
	12	•	6.5	24	10†	•	•	•	•	•	•	•	•

(Adapted from: FHA Pole House Construction, AWPI.)

•Embedment depth is greater than eight feet, considered excessively expensive.
†These tip diameters may be decreased one inch, provided embedment is increased by one-half foot.

H = Unsupported height of uphill pole.
A = Embedment depth, using backfill of tamped earth, sand, gravel, or crushed rock.
B = Embedment depth, using backfill of concrete or soil/cement.
D = Bearing diameter.

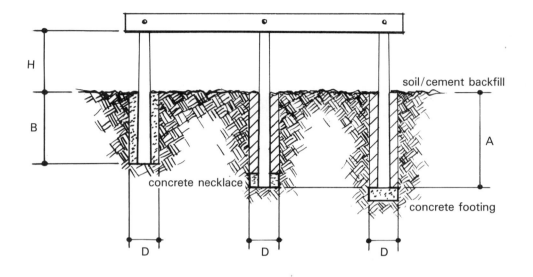

soil/cement backfill

concrete necklace

concrete footing

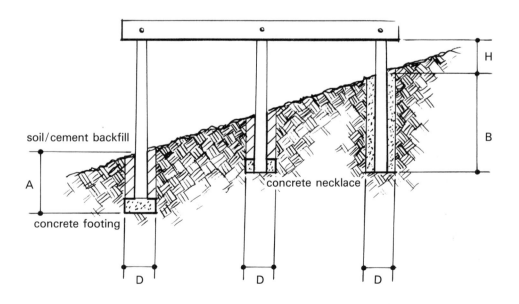

soil/cement backfill

concrete necklace

concrete footing

Hole Excavation

There are several ways to excavate the holes for the poles. To avoid damaging the site vegetation, holes are often dug by hand with the aid of a breaker bar and post hole digger. The *breaker bar* allows you to break up hard-packed soil and small rocks which can then be lifted out with the post hole digger. A *post hole digger* is an absolutely necessary tool if you want to dig a 16-inch hole down 5 feet. Using a shovel, you would end up with a small pit and wouldn't be able to pour a uniform concrete necklace around the pole.

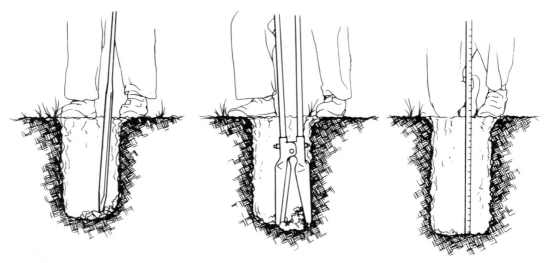

Figure 5–3. Use a breaker bar to loosen soil and rocks, remove debris with a post hole digger, and check with a tape measure to make sure hole is below frost line and at proper embedment depth.

Power augers can also be used for excavation. A small tractor with an auger attachment can dig cylindrical holes quickly and without much site disruption. A backhoe can be used, but again you end up with large pits rather than properly-sized holes.

Refer to tables 5–3 through 5–6 for the proper hole diameter, "*D*." For example, 18 inches is the minimum diameter suggested. This leaves room for a 5-inch wide concrete necklace around a class 5 pole that has an 8-inch butt diameter. After the holes are dug, re-attach the string lines to make sure the center of the holes are where you want them and use a plumb bob to make sure the hole walls are vertical.

Pole Embedment

Pole raising can usually be done with several strong people simply standing the pole upright and dropping it into its hole. If you are working alone or dealing with 30-foot poles, you will want to set

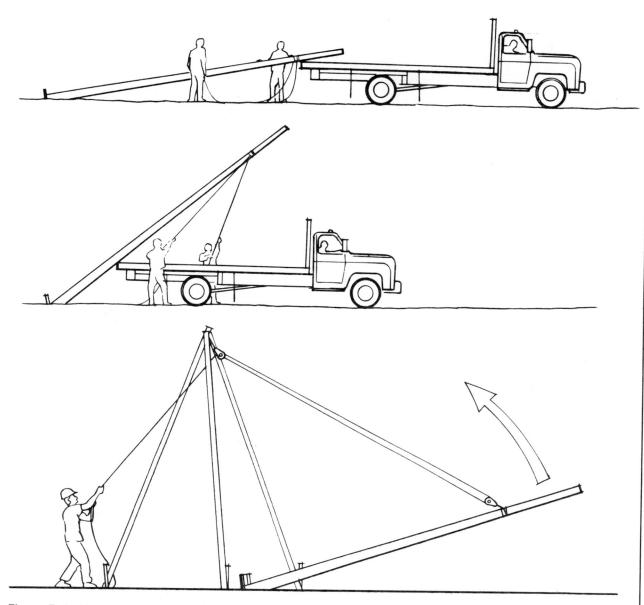

Figure 5-4. Here are two methods of hoisting large poles into place. For large building projects, a pole truck with a mechanical arm could be rented for a day.

up a block and tackle arrangement to mechanically hoist the poles into place.

Whichever method you use, make sure you have stakes and bracing on hand to adequately secure the pole once it is upright. You will also want to have a set of boards that can be put in the hole for the pole to slide against in order to protect the dirt wall of the hole. A wall protector can easily be made out of four 1×4 boards that are fastened together with strips of metal on the back, such as aluminum flashing, so the boards can hinge to fit the contours of the hole. This will keep dirt from being gouged out of the side wall and getting under the pole which reduces the hole's bearing capacity.

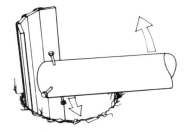

Figure 5-5. Protector boards such as these will keep the pole from gouging the dirt walls and filling in the hole.

From tree to pole, a neighborhood barn raising using freshly cut cedar. First the holes are dug while the bark is stripped off the cedar poles. The poles are measured for straightness with a chalk line and the best ones selected for the corners of the building. The poles are set into the holes by hand and then plumbed. With the pole exactly positioned and plumb, bracing is attached to keep it from moving.

Pole Raising

The first step in pole raising is to sort out all your poles according to straightness and length. Use a chalkline held against the pole to determine which ones are the straightest. You will want to use these for the corners of the building which must be plumb in two directions. You also will want to use the longest poles on the downhill side of the building or in the deepest holes, where a few extra inches in length might make a difference in reaching the rafter girts. When the poles are sorted out, reattach the building line strings and raise each pole as follows:

- Slip the wall protector boards in the first hole and position the butt of the pole against them. Screw in several lag screws 6 inches up from the bottom to tie in the concrete necklace, and then lower the pole into the hole.
- Use a 4-foot level to plumb the pole while your helpers hold it upright, and then use a tape measure to check the distance between the pole and your building lines. With a sledge hammer, gently tap the pole to move the bottom in the hole, so you get the proper distance to your building lines. Now check to be sure the pole is plumb again. If the poles are in the walls of the building, you will want to plumb the outer edge of the pole so the siding girts will be plumb. If the pole is outside or inside the walls, you can plumb the centerline of the pole.
- When you have the pole where you want it, attach two pieces of 2 × 4 or 2 × 6 bracing to the pole to keep it plumb. The bracing should run both with the wall line and at right angles to the wall line in order to brace the pole in both possible directions of movement. Nail the bracing onto the pole and then into a stake driven into the ground. Use 16d nails that are not quite driven in all the way, so they can be easily removed later on. Before driving your final nails into the stakes, however, make sure the pole is still plumb.

If the poles are in the walls, the straightness of the corner poles is critical. They must have two plumb surfaces, something that is a bit of a trick finding with tappered, irregular poles. Do your best using the level and your eyesight to compensate for bows and bends in the pole. Remember that it is always easier to shim out a pole surface that has bowed in rather than cut back one that protrudes past the building envelope.

Concrete Necklace

Contrary to popular thought, placing a concrete pad under the pole is not the most effective way to increase its bearing strength. According to pole engineers, a *necklace* of concrete poured around the pole increases its bearing strength considerably

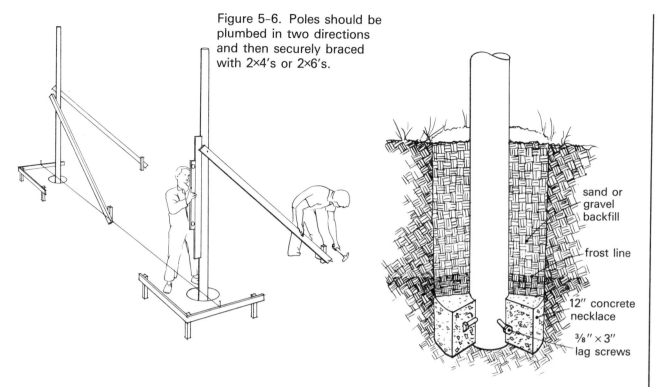

Figure 5-6. Poles should be plumbed in two directions and then securely braced with 2×4's or 2×6's.

sand or gravel backfill

frost line

12" concrete necklace

$3/8'' \times 3''$ lag screws

Figure 5-7. Pole embedment details.

more. This is because the majority of the vertical load is transmitted to the soil by skin friction with the pole. Thus, increasing the surface area contact with a concrete necklace improves both the pole's vertical and lateral loadbearing ability.

For poles in average to good soils at the proper embedment depth, a 12-inch concrete necklace poured below the frost line should be used. Lag screws should be embedded in the bottom of the pole to help tie the pole and concrete necklace together as shown in figure 5-7.

For poles in below average soils or poles that are at less than the specified embedment depth, a full necklace of an earth/cement mixture can serve to increase the bearing capacity of the pole. Soil should be put through a 1-inch screen to remove large stones and then mixed with cement in a ratio of 5 parts soil to 1 part cement. This mixture is almost as strong as concrete for the purposes of a necklace and is considerably cheaper. Fill the entire hole up to within several inches of the surface with this mixture, using lag screws along the pole to secure it to the necklace.

Increasing Pole Rigidity. If you cannot achieve the pole embedment depth recommended in the charts because of bedrock or other obstacles, there are two ways to increase the rigidity of shallow poles. The first is to pour a concrete necklace around the pole up to grade which increases its bearing surface. This is effective in cases where say a 5-foot embedment is recommended but you hit undiggable hardpan at 4 feet. Where you hit bedrock at 1 foot down, *diagonal bracing* between the poles is the only way to lock the poles into a rigid structure. Figure 5–8 shows how diagonal bracing can be used for shallow pole foundations.

Backfilling

After the concrete necklaces have been poured and allowed to set up for several hours, the holes can be backfilled. Sand or

Figure 5–8. Three methods of bracing poles when the required embedment depth cannot be achieved.

Working with Concrete

In pole building, only a small amount of concrete is needed for the necklaces around poles. Additional concrete might be needed if you are building a chimney or stairs that need a foundation under them.

Concrete is made up of sand and gravel held together with Portland cement. The usual ratio of these ingredients is 1 part Portland cement, 2½ parts sand, and 3½ parts gravel. The sand should be free of debris, and ¾-inch crushed stone or equivalent size graded rock used for the gravel.

Concrete is measured by the cubic yard, a volume measuring $3 \times 3 \times 3$ feet or 27 cubic feet. Thus a slab of concrete that measures 18×18 feet and is 4 inches thick would be:

$$\text{Volume} = \frac{18 \times 18 \times \frac{1}{3}}{27} = \frac{108}{27} = 4 \text{ cubic yards (cuy)}$$

To figure the amount of concrete that must be used for a necklace around a pole, use the formula for the area of a circle: pi(3.14) × radius² × the depth of the necklace to get its volume. We must then subtract the volume of the pole. If we poured an 18-inch diameter by 12-inch deep necklace around an 8-inch pole, our calculations would be as follows:

$$\text{Volume} = \frac{3.14 \times 81 \times 12}{(12 \times 12 \times 12)} = 1.77 \text{ cu. ft.}$$

$$\text{Less pole volume} = \frac{3.14 \times 16 \times 12}{(12 \times 12 \times 12)} = .35 \text{ cu. ft.}$$

$$\begin{array}{l}\text{Volume} \\ \text{of necklace}\end{array} = 1.77 - .35 = 1.42 \text{ cu. ft.} = \frac{1.42}{27} = .05 \text{ cubic yards}$$

You can mix your own concrete from the raw ingredients, buy pre-mixed 80-pound bags, or order ready-mix concrete delivered by a truck. If you are using less than ½-cubic yard, it makes sense to buy it in 80-pound bags and simply mix it in a wheelbarrow or cement mixer. Over ½-cubic yard, it pays to mix your own or call a concrete truck in, since you would need about 50 pre-mixed bags just to get 1 cubic yard.

When you are working with concrete, always wear protective rubber gloves and rubber boots. Concrete is very abrasive and caustic, and will make short work of your hands and leather work boots if they are unprotected.

This pole house uses both tie rod bracing between poles and large concrete necklaces around the poles to brace the pole frame.

crushed stone is the best backfill material since it will not hold water, freeze, and then heave. Good soil with a low clay content can also be used. For poles embedded in poor soils, a backfill of soil/cement mixture is recommended as outlined above.

Since the concrete necklaces have not totally hardened after only a few hours, backfill the holes very gently. The backfill will sit on top of the concrete and slow down the drying process making for stronger concrete. The next day come back and flood the backfill with water to make sure the sand or soil is completely compacted.

The poles are now completely self-supporting, but it is a good idea to leave the bracing on the poles until it must come off for the framing.

POLE FRAMING AND JOINTRY

CHAPTER SIX

There are several ways to frame pole buildings. The choice of technique depends on design considerations such as loads, choice of siding, insulation levels, and aesthetics. This chapter shows the standard framing techniques and fasteners that have been tried and proven in the field.

Fasteners

Nails

The lowly nail is still the basic fastener used in carpentry despite the advent of power staple guns, metal clips, and super-strength glues. Nails are measured by the *penny* which is abbreviated "*d*." Figure 6–1 shows common nail sizes, their length and their shank diameter.

There are four basic types of nails: common, box, finish, and casement. There are also spiral and ring shank nails that are used for special purposes. *Common nails* are used for conventional framing and Appendix I shows what sizes are recommended for various aspects of platform construction. *Box nails* are like common nails, except their shank is thinner, making them good for nailing trim or other wood that might split. *Finish nails* have a thin shank like box nails and have almost no head at all, allowing them to be sunk and puttied over for finish work. *Casement nails* are similar to finish nails but have a slightly larger head for better holding power. All of these nails are available with a galvanized coating making them rust-proof for exterior work.

Ring shank nails have annular or spiral grooves on their shank to resist withdrawal. The *pole spike* or *barn spike* is a ringed nail used to attach girts to poles. It is made of hardened steel and comes in lengths up to 8 inches long. Spiral or ringed nails are also used for metal roofing, flooring, drywall, and other special applications.

Choosing nails. There are two types of forces on a nail. The first is shear or downward force trying to break the shank of the nail and the other is withdrawal force trying to pull the nail out. In pole building, withdrawal is of primary concern since the girt

Figure 6-1. Nail types and sizes.

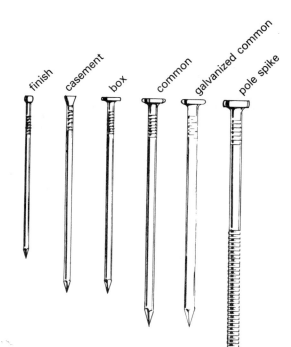

Table 6-1

NAIL SIZE AND NUMBER PER POUND

Size	Length (in.)	Common		Box	
		Diameter (in.)	No. per Pound	Diameter (in.)	No. per Pound
4d	1-1/2	.102	316	.083	473
5d	1-3/4	.102	271	.083	406
6d	2	.115	181	.102	236
7d	2-1/4	.115	161	.102	210
8d	2-1/2	.131	106	.115	145
10d	3	.148	69	.127	94
12d	3-1/4	.148	63	.127	88
16d	3-1/2	.165	49	.134	71
20d	4	.203	31	.148	52
30d	4-1/2	.220	24	.148	46
40d	5	.238	18	.165	35

in pole connection is constantly being twisted and moved by wind loading and other forces. This could lead to gradual withdrawal and weakening of the connection. **Pole spikes effectively resist this withdrawal force and therefore are the only type of nail recommended for securing girts to poles.**

A nail's resistance to withdrawal is dependent on its surface friction with the wood. Therefore, a nail of twice the diameter of another has twice the holding power. Galvanized nails hold better than common nails because of their rough surface. When framing with green, unseasoned lumber, always use galvanized nails to resist rusting and to counteract the shrinking of the wood from around the nail as it dries. Appendix I lists nailing patterns for platform framing.

Bolted Connections

Most pole buildings, especially larger ones, use lag screws, bolts or threaded rods to secure girts to the poles. *Lag screws* are used when the girts are only on one side of the pole. If there are girts on both sides, then they can be bolted together through the pole. *Threaded bolts or rods* have a large diameter shank to resist sheer forces and cannot pull out of the wood at all.

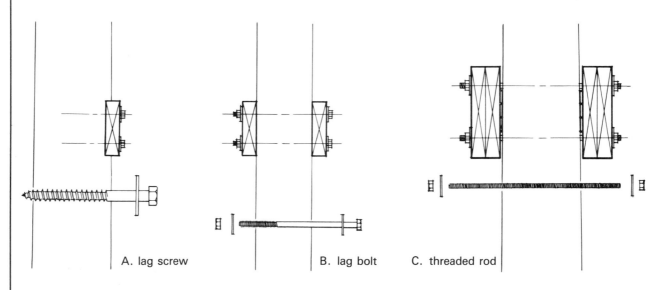

A. lag screw   B. lag bolt   C. threaded rod

Figure 6-2. Three types of threaded girt connectors.

Lag screws, bolts and rods are measured by the diameter and length of their shank. Half-inch-diameter bolts are a common size for attaching girts to poles. If the shank of a bolt is too short to get through the pole, then a threaded rod can be used that can be cut to any length. Washers should always be used on bolted connections to distribute the clamping force, so the wood does not collapse under the bolt head.

One problem with bolted connections is that all the force is concentrated on the small area of the bolt hole rather than distributed across the entire joint. Various types of spiked grids and split ring connectors are available to meet this problem by providing a bigger bearing area.

For attaching girts to poles, there is a curved *spike grid* that fits the shape of the pole so that no notching is necessary. As the girt is tightened to the pole, the teeth of the spike grid embed in both the pole and girt forming a large area of contact. *Flat grids* are also available for attaching girts to square posts or other dimensioned lumber.

Another type of connector is the *toothed ring connector* which is smaller and is completely embedded in the wood when the joint is pulled together. The *split ring connector* is similar and slightly stronger, but requires the pieces to be drilled out to accept the ring

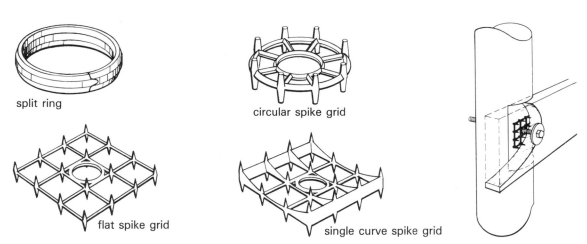

split ring

circular spike grid

flat spike grid

single curve spike grid

Figure 6-3. Split ring and spike grid connectors.

before it is assembled. Figure 6–5 shows the relative strengths of a nailed joint versus a bolted joint and one with a connector.

Framing Anchors

Floors, walls, and the roof are often framed conventionally with studs, joists, and rafters in pole construction. There is a wide variety of connectors available to make this job easier, stronger, and more economical.

The principal connector that is almost always used is the *joist hanger*. These hangers allow joists to be set flush with the girts or carrying beams.

Flat plate connectors are another handy item for putting together roof trusses or splicing beams together. Figure 6–4 shows these and other connectors and their uses.

Figure 6-4. Framing anchors and connectors.

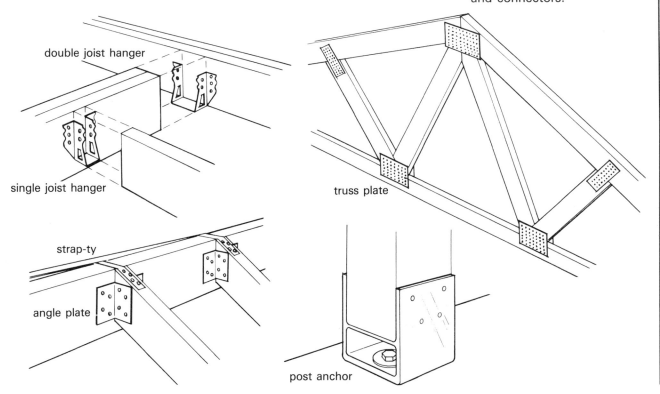

double joist hanger

single joist hanger

strap-ty

angle plate

truss plate

post anchor

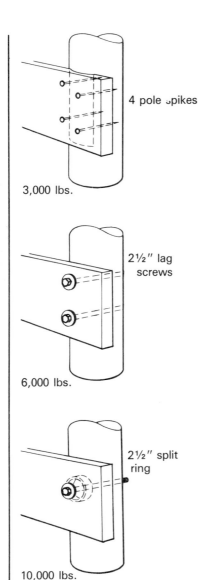

4 pole spikes

3,000 lbs.

2½" lag screws

6,000 lbs.

2½" split ring

10,000 lbs.

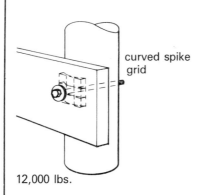

curved spike grid

12,000 lbs.

Figure 6-5. The relative strength of different connectors. Actual carrying capacity depends on species and quality of wood as well as orientation of grain.

What Connector to Use

The type of girt to pole connections you should use depends on what type of girts you are attaching and how big a load they are carrying. There are no simple ways to determine the exact connector size for a given girt without getting into a lot of engineering calculations, but there are some general rules of thumb.

Siding girts, because of their small loads, can be nailed in place with pole spikes. Preferably, the poles are slightly notched to give a flat bearing surface and the girt is attached with 4 pole spikes. Notching is not always necessary, however, and you can usually do without it by driving a few extra spikes into the pole.

Floor and rafter girts should be secured with ½-inch lag screws, bolts, or threaded rods. Notching is not necessary, but helps to give a better bearing surface and strengthen the joint. When using lag screws, always predrill the girt with a hole that is the same size as the bolt shank; predrill the pole with a hole that is slightly smaller than the root size of the threads. With any type of lag screw or bolt, always use a large steel washer to distribute the loading around the bolt head.

The strongest type of joint is achieved by using a spiked grid connector that distributes the strain evenly onto the pole and girt. As shown in figure 6–5 a spiked grid connector has double the bearing capacity of two ½-inch bolts. Such connectors are usually not necessary for small pole buildings that have relatively close pole spacing, but should be considered for long girt spans in larger buildings where the load on the connection may exceed 6,000 pounds.

Girt Framing

A normal sequence of pole building is to set the poles, attach all the girts, frame in the floors and walls, and then frame and finish the roof. Often, however, it makes sense to frame and finish the roof first, once the girts have been set. This allows you to finish the construction under cover and to minimize water damage to framing and subflooring. If you are facing inclement weather during construction, this advantage of pole building should always be considered.

Attaching Girts

There are several methods of attaching the girts depending on what type of fastener you are using.

The simplest method is to notch the pole and use pole spikes to attach the girt. Notching the pole is necessary to give a flat nailing surface for the girt to butt against in order to maintain the strength of the nailed joint. These notches can be made with a hatchet and a circular saw with the blade set to about 1-inch depth.

Simply make a series of cuts across the pole where the notch should be and chisel out the waste wood with the hatchet. Notches should be just deep enough to form about a 4-inch flat nailing surface and should be treated with a wood preservative before the girts are attached.

The disadvantages of notching are that it takes time and slightly weakens the pole and its preservative shell. Wielding a saw 20 feet in the air can also be a bit dangerous. To avoid notching, girts can be bolted onto the poles directly or with spike grid connectors. Setting blocks should be nailed onto the poles to temporarily hold the girt at the proper level, and then the girt and the pole can be drilled for bolts.

Floor Girts

The first girts to go on, if there are framed floors in the building, are the floor girts. The bottom of the first floor girts should be set a minimum of 8 inches off the ground to keep them away from moisture and insects at ground level. Later, a sill girt will be put on to close off the bottom of the building. If the poles are set outside the building envelope, then the floor girts should be from pressure-treated lumber, since they will extend unprotected from the building.

A level girt line. The first step in setting the floor girts is to mark a level line that corresponds to the bottom of the girts on all the poles. This can be done with a string and line level. Starting at the corner that has the highest ground level, mark where the bottom of the girt will be. If you are building a floor close to the ground, the minimum distance from the earth to the bottom of the framing should be 8 inches as mentioned above. Attach the string to a nail driven into the corner pole, and, using the line level, continue from pole to pole using a nail to mark the bottom of the girts.

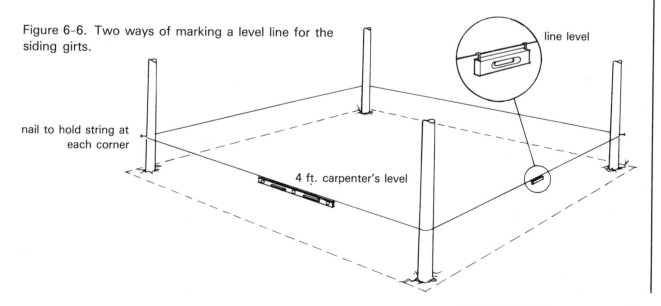

Figure 6-6. Two ways of marking a level line for the siding girts.

line level

nail to hold string at each corner

4 ft. carpenter's level

If, when you come back to your original mark, you are still right on level, you've done a good job. If you're off, go back and check the lines between poles again, perhaps using a 4-foot carpenter's level to check the strings to see whether your line level is accurate. It is very important that the first set of girts be dead level, not only to give you a good floor, but so all your other girts will be level, since their heights will be measured from these girts.

To bolt the girts in place, nail temporary setting blocks flush to the mark that shows the bottom of the girt. The girts can sit on these while they are drilled and bolted into place.

Siding Girts

The siding girts should be installed next, if they are necessary. Many heated and insulated pole buildings have regularly framed walls with 2 × 4s or 2 × 6s to hold insulation and carry the siding, but most barns and outbuildings use girts to carry the siding. Siding girts need only be large enough to support the siding weight. Usually, 2 × 6s spaced 2 feet apart vertically are all that is necessary for vertical board or panel siding.

Table 6–2 lists safe spans for siding girts under moderate wind loading when placed 24 and 48 inches on center (o.c.). As can be seen from the table, an effective way to boost the strength of siding girts is to add a horizontal 2 × 4 or 2 × 6 brace nailed at right angles to the girt. Such a brace can increase the effective span of a siding girt and also serve as interior framing for insulation and wall covering.

The *sill girt* is a special siding girt that is usually a pressure-treated 2 × 10 which is nailed onto the poles at ground level with its bottom edge just slightly buried in the soil. The top of the girt, at 8 inches off the ground, will serve as a nailer for the bottom of the siding; the rest of it will serve to close off the bottom of the pole

Table 6–2

SIDING GIRT SPANS

Girt Size	Spacing	Maximum Span
2 × 4	2' o.c.	8'
	4' o.c.	5'-6"
2 × 6	2' o.c.	13'
	4' o.c.	9'
2 × 6 with	2' o.c.	16'
2 × 6 brace	4' o.c.	12'-6"

Fiber bending stress (Fb) = 1450 lbs.
wind loading = 15 lbs. per sq. ft.

building, acting as a splash board so it gets wet instead of the siding.

Normal siding girts start 24 inches above the sill girt and continue on up, usually 24 inches on center (o.c.). They are attached with pole spikes and may be notched into the pole for better bearing strength and straightness.

While it is not absolutely necessary for siding girts to be dead level, it is important that they do form a vertical plane for the siding. Normally, the outsides of the poles are set plumb, so their taper does not effect the siding. Occasionally, there will be crooked poles where it will be necessary to either notch the girt in or shim it out from the pole in order to get a good siding surface. Keep checking the siding girts with a 4-foot level and tight string to detect and correct any bows as the girts are attached.

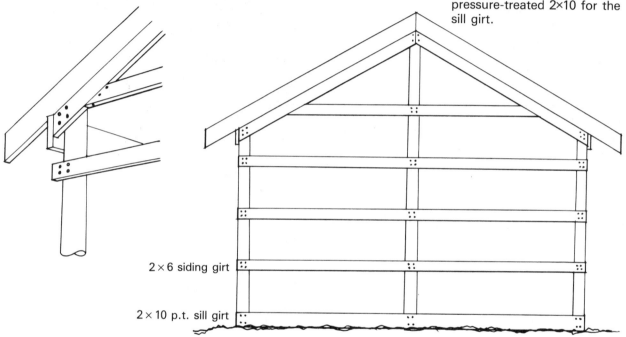

Figure 6-7. Siding girts 24 inches on center with a pressure-treated 2×10 for the sill girt.

2 × 6 siding girt

2 × 10 p.t. sill girt

Rafter Girts

The rafter girts are the final ones to be attached and can go on in several different ways. On a gable roof there are two different sets of girts. There is the *ridge girt* which carries the rafters at the top of the roof and the *eave girt* which supports the bottom of the rafter.

The eave girts, which are normally double 2 × 10s or larger, can go on in two different ways. The double girt can be spiked together and bolted on the outside of the poles, or the single 2 × 10s can be put on either side of the pole in the same manner as floor girts. With a double eave girt on the outside, the *bird's mouth cut* of the rafter sits right on the girt, just as it would sit on a plate in conventional construction. When the double girt is broken up and

The weekend barn raising continues with the installation of the siding girts. First, the poles are scored with a circular saw set to a 1-inch depth and then the cut is cleaned out with a hatchet. The conscientious use of eye and ear protectors will prevent possible eye damage from flying wood chips and the gradual high-frequency hearing loss associated with the use of circular saws.

The girt is then temporarily tacked in place and checked for plumb. Finally, it is shimmed out or recessed as necessary and nailed in place with pole spikes.

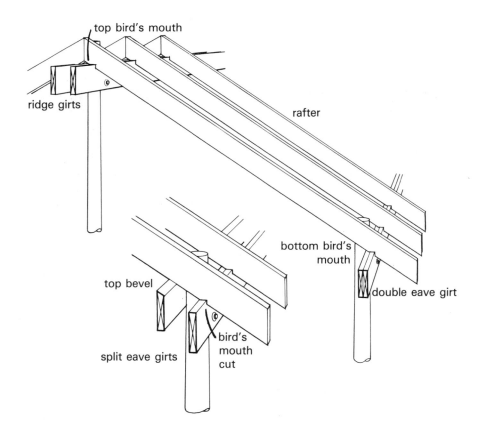

Figure 6-8. Eave and ridge girt framing.

put on either side of the pole, however, a problem arises since the two girts must be at different heights to match the slope of the roof rafters.

The solution is to only set the outside girts before the roof is framed. The inside ones can then be pushed tight against the rafters after they are in place. The edge of the inside girt can be beveled at the roof angle to butt tightly against the rafters and avoid having to make a second series of bird's mouth cuts on the rafters. The single outside girt will be able to temporarily carry the weight of the rafters, but the inside girt should be installed before the roof decking and covering are installed.

If a ridge girt is used, it goes on like a floor girt on either side of the center poles and the rafter is notched with a bird's mouth to fit over it.

Girt framing for other types of roofs, such as shed and hip roofs, is essentially the same. For a shed roof there are two eave girts on the front and back of the building and no ridge girt. For a hip roof, there are four eave girts on each side of the building to catch the bottom of the rafters and again no ridge girt. A gambrel roof is similar to a gable; it has two eave girts and an optional ridge girt at the peak of the roof.

When all the rafter girts are on, you will want to trim off the top of the poles, so they don't stick up above the rafters. Use a circular saw and hand saw, or chain saw to trim the poles so they are just below the top of the rafters. You should leave enough of the pole sticking up to nail adjacent rafters to it.

Rafter Framing

With all the girts in place, you can start framing either at the top or bottom. As mentioned before, it often makes sense to frame the roof first and cover it to protect the building. If having the floors framed in makes it considerably easier to work on the roof, then you might want to start framing bottom up. It's one of the flexible options you have in pole construction.

On the following pages are illustrations of the framing details for four types of conventional roofs that might be put on a pole building. As can be seen, the framing details are almost exactly like conventional stick framing with rafters set 16 or 24 inches on center (o.c.). The major differences are that the rafters rest on an eave girt rather than a wall plate, and a ridge girt replaces the ridge board in a gable roof.

Figure 6-10 shows how rafters are laid out and how the various cuts are made by stepping-off the rafter with a framing square. Consult the rafter span table in chapter 4 to select the proper size rafter for your particular building.

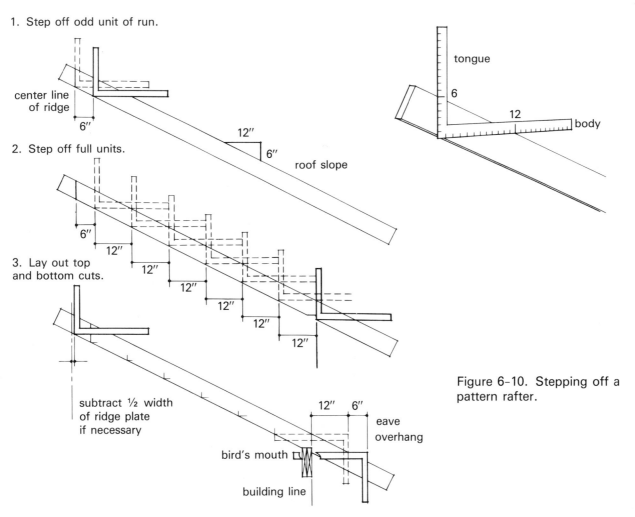

Figure 6-10. Stepping off a pattern rafter.

Laying Out Rafters

There are 2 methods of laying out the cut lines on rafters. The first is trial and error by marking the rafter in place. The second is by using a rafter square and stepping off the rise and run of the roof on the rafter.

Holding a piece of lumber in place and trying to eyeball the cuts is not recommended unless you are framing a gable roof that has a ridge girt. With a ridge and eave girt to rest the rafter on, it is easy to mark the bird's mouth cuts at top and bottom which will allow the rafter to sit on both girts. This is the same technique that is used on a shed roof. Simply put a piece of lumber in place, mark it for length and the position of the bird's mouth cuts, cut it, test it in place again and then use it for a template to cut the other rafters.

Framing a gable roof with no ridge girt, however, requires that you use a rafter square since there is no practical way to hold the rafter in place while you mark it.

First get to know your rafter square. It has a 2-foot long, large side that is called the *body*. The other smaller side is called the *tongue*. For calculating the length of a rafter, we will use the body to represent the horizontal run of the roof and the tongue to represent the vertical rise. Figure 6–10 shows how to step off a rafter for a roof that has a slope of 6:12. The run of the roof is 6′ 6″ from the center of the roofline to the outside edge of the eave girt.

Pick a straight piece of lumber to be the pattern rafter, and starting at the top, place the square on the rafter so the 6-inch mark on the tongue and the 12-inch mark on the body line up with the top edge of the rafter. Make a mark along the back edge of the tongue; this marks the top plumb cut at the ridgeline. You will have to subtract half the width of the ridge board from this line to compensate for its thickness.

Next, step off the odd unit of run, in this case 6 inches, by making a mark at 6 inches on the body. Slide the square down the rafter, still in the 6:12 position, until the back of the tongue lines up with this mark. Now you can step off six full 12-inch increments of run by making a mark at 12 inches on the body and then moving the tongue down to this mark, keeping the square in the 6:12 position.

The last mark you make will indicate the outside of the rafter girt and this is the back edge of the bird's mouth cut. To mark this cut, simply turn the square over; line up the 12-inch mark on the body and the 6-inch mark on the tongue on the top edge of the rafter; draw a line along the bottom edge of the body when it measures the same width as the rafter girt.

To mark the eave overhang you can continue moving the square down one full 12-inch length and then a 6-inch length to get a 1½-foot overhang. Often it is more accurate to mark and cut the tail cut on the bottom of the rafter after the rafter is in place. If the eave girt bends up or down, in or out, along its length, then pre-made tail cuts won't form a straight line for the fascia board. I prefer to use a chalk line on the rafters after they are in place to get an absolutely straight line for the fascia.

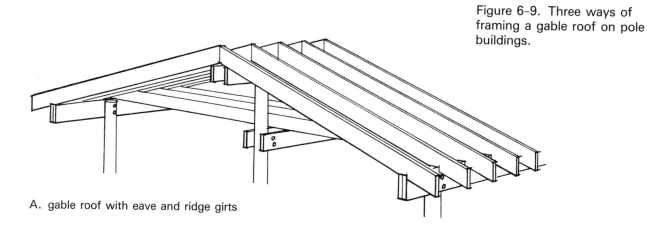

Figure 6-9. Three ways of framing a gable roof on pole buildings.

A. gable roof with eave and ridge girts

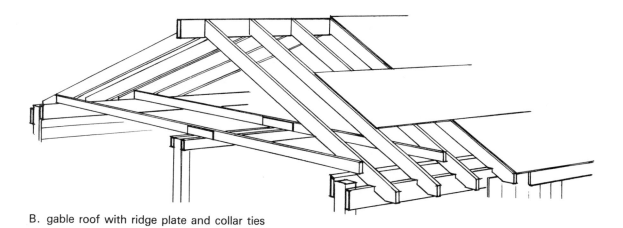

B. gable roof with ridge plate and collar ties

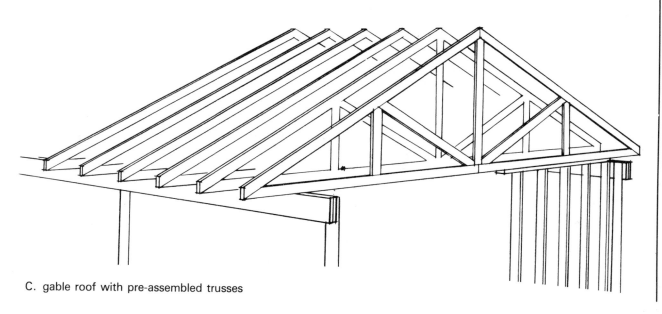

C. gable roof with pre-assembled trusses

Gable Roof

In gable roof construction, the rafters are notched with a bird's mouth cut on the top and bottom to fit over the girts. Since the inside eave girt is put in place after the rafters, simply bevel the edge of it so it has a good bearing surface against the rafters. Don't bother to make a third set of bird's mouth cuts.

Use the stepping-off method to make the plumb and bird's mouth cuts on the rafter, but wait until all the rafters are in place before making the tail cut. You can then use a chalkline stretched tight from one end of the building to the other to mark the top of the tail cut. Use an angle gauge to mark a plumb line on each rafter down from the chalk line and then cut off each rafter. This will give you a perfectly straight surface for nailing the fascia board.

In gable roof framing, it is not absolutely necessary to have a ridge girt, nor to extend the middle poles up to the top of the roof. If a pole building is using free-standing framed walls, then all the poles could be cut off at the top of the walls, and a standard gable roof with ridge plate could be set on top of the eave girts. By extending the middle poles to the ridge and using a ridge girt, however, the strength of the roof both for snow and wind loading is greatly increased, since the rafters are tied directly into the pole frame.

In pole construction, use of collar ties to triangulate pairs of rafters to keep the side walls from bowing out is usually not necessary. The poles are able to resist the lateral force of the roof, and the ridge girt keeps the ridge from sagging and putting pressure on the side walls. This means that attic space in pole buildings is more open and usable.

Using trusses. Manufactured roof trusses are another way to frame a gable roof and can cut labor costs significantly. Because trusses can be built out of smaller lumber than normal rafters, their delivered cost is usually only slightly more than the material cost for normal framing. Also, they can be nailed directly in place, saving the labor of making bird's mouth, plumb, and tail cuts on each individual rafter. A ridge girt cannot be used with a truss system, and therefore temporary 1×3 strapping must be used to tie the trusses together, in order to keep them from blowing over while they are being erected.

Hip Roof

Hip roof construction is similar to gable roof framing except there are four different roof planes and two different kinds of rafters. There are 4 hip rafters which run at an angle and rest on the corner poles. These support jack rafters 16 or 24 inches on center (o.c.). The *jack rafters* are similar to common rafters except the top

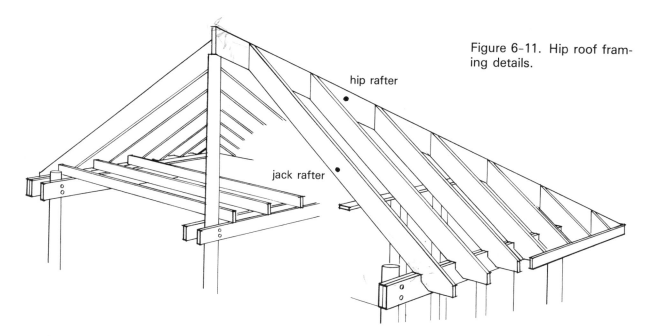

Figure 6-11. Hip roof framing details.

hip rafter

jack rafter

plumb cut must be beveled to meet the hip rafter. Most framing squares have a special table on them for figuring the common difference in length for jack rafters, given their spacing and the slope of the roof. This distance can simply be added to the next jack rafter to have it meet the hip rafter at the correct spacing.

Shed Roof

A shed roof is perhaps the simplest kind of roof to build. The rafters are simply laid on top of the girts with a bird's mouth cut for the two outside girts. The front and back tail cuts are made after the rafters are in place to give a good, straight line for the fascia. If there are intermediate supporting girts for shed roof rafters, they should be put on after the rafters are in place with a beveled edge to butt tight against the bottom of the rafters.

1 × 3 strapping, 24″ o.c.

Figure 6-12. Shed roof framing details.

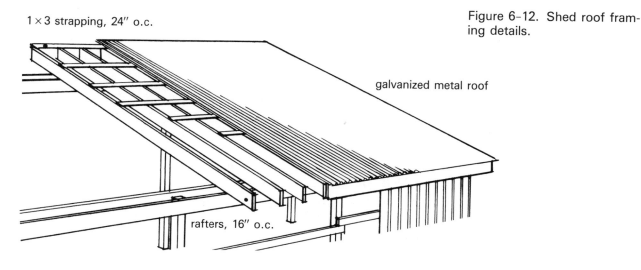

galvanized metal roof

rafters, 16″ o.c.

Gambrel Roof

The gambrel roof is often used for barns, because it increases storage space under the rafters. A simple gambrel roof can be put together using plywood gussets to join the rafter pieces together. Figure 6–13 shows the nailing and gluing details for joining rafters with plywood gussets. The top ridge girt is optional for both gambrel and gable roofs, but does add considerably to the rigidity and strength of the roof system.

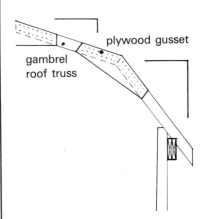

Figure 6-13. Gambrel roof framing details.

gambrel roof truss

plywood gusset

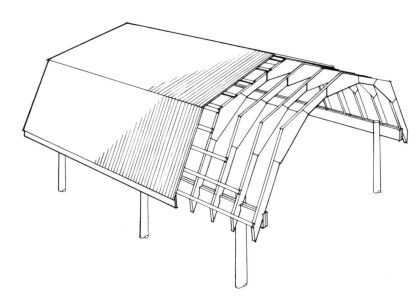

Cutting the Rafter Tails in Place

The tail cut on a rafter can be made before it is put in place or after all the rafters are in place. I prefer to make this cut after the rafters are in place, so I know I will have a straight line for the fascia board.

To cut the rafters in place, first measure out from the building framing the width of your eave overhang and make a mark on the two rake rafters at either end of the building. Then take a chalk line, stretch it across the tops of all the rafters connecting these two points, and snap a line. This line marks the top of the tail cuts. Next, take a 2-foot level and draw a plumb line down from the chalk mark on one of the rafters. Set an adjustable angle guide on top of the rafter and set it to the angle of this line. You can now use the angle guide to mark the tail cut on all the other rafters.

Make the tail cuts with a circular saw, working from below, off a ladder or staging. You will now have a perfectly straight nailing surface for the fascia board which will save you time and frustration when it comes to doing the trim work.

Rafter and Purlin

Another type of roof framing, used on large pole buildings, is post and beam framing which utilizes large rafter beams set 4 feet or more apart to carry thick roof decking or stress-skin panels. The rafters are attached directly to the poles and the intermediate spans are broken up with purlins that span from rafter to rafter as necessary to carry the decking. Figure 6–14 shows two post and beam roof systems, one with purlins.

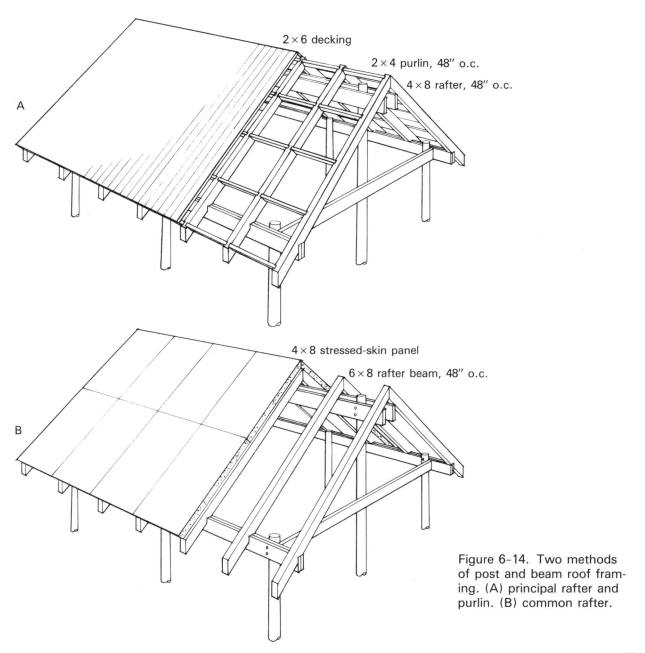

2 × 6 decking

2 × 4 purlin, 48" o.c.

4 × 8 rafter, 48" o.c.

A

4 × 8 stressed-skin panel

6 × 8 rafter beam, 48" o.c.

B

Figure 6-14. Two methods of post and beam roof framing. (A) principal rafter and purlin. (B) common rafter.

Eave Framing

The roof overhangs on a building, called *eaves*, are an important but often confusing part of roof framing. Eaves are important to keep water off the siding and away from the foundation. They can also serve as shading devices to keep the summer sun off windows.

On the walls where the rafters sit, the eave is formed by the extension of the rafter and a *lookout* which returns horizontally to the house wall. A *fascia* board is attached to the tail cut on the rafters and a *soffit* board is attached underneath to the lookouts. The lookouts can be eliminated and the soffit simply attached to the underside of the rafters to form a sloping soffit detail.

The eaves on the gable ends of a building are called *rakes*. There are two methods of framing rakes in pole building. The first is to simply extend the eave girts past the building frame to carry the rake rafter. The length that the girt extends past the building will be determined by the width of the soffit.

Figure 6-15. Two methods of eave framing. (A) horizontal soffit detail. (B) sloping soffit detail.

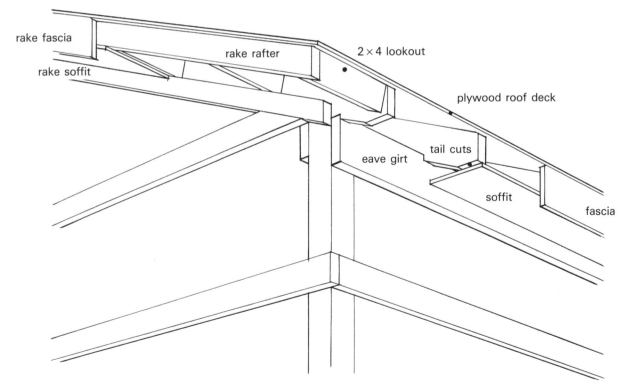

A. horizontal soffit

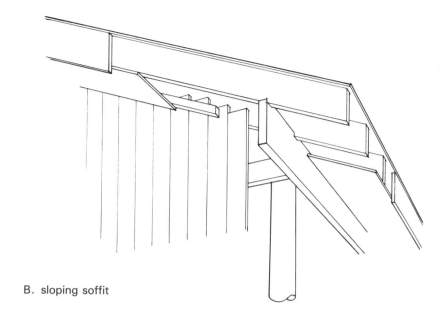

B. sloping soffit

The second method is the rake detail that is used in conventional framing. The eave girts stop at the building line and 2 × 4 lookouts extending to a 2 × 4 rake rafter are framed from the end rafter to carry the rake overhang. If the overhang is 12 inches or less, the 2 × 4s can be nailed directly to the end rafter and stiffened up by securely nailing it to the roof decking that will be put on next. If the overhang is wider than 12 inches, the 2 × 4 lookouts should cantilever over a cut-down end rafter and extend back to the second to last rafter to give it more support.

The first method of simply extending the eave girts to support a rake rafter is very simple but poses some finishing problems for houses or other buildings that have a conventional flat soffit. The problem is that the rake rafter and therefore the fascia board that will cover it is much wider than the fascia board that will go on the tail cuts of the rafters. This simply means the rake eaves will appear larger and heavier than the other eaves. This is not really a problem if the rafters are 2 × 6s, since a 1 × 8 fascia board would work and not appear too wide. On 2 × 12 rafters, however, the width of the rake fascia would be very noticeable indeed.

Figure 6–15 shows the construction details for both types of eave framing. When the roof framing is complete, it should be decked and then covered with roofing as soon as possible. Chapter 7 covers different methods and materials for roofing as well as details on finishing off the eaves.

Floor and Wall Framing

Floor and wall framing on pole buildings is again similar to conventional stick framing, using 2-inch dimensioned lumber 16 or 24 inches on center (o.c.). Consult the joist table in chapter 4 to determine safe joist spans.

Joist Framing

Joists can either rest on top of the floor girts or be suspended between them with joist hangers. Both methods have advantages and disadvantages.

Setting the joists on top of the girts eliminates the expense of joist hangers but requires additional lumber for the headers that tie the ends of the joists together. This method, illustrated in figure 6–16, is always used when the joists are cantilevered over the girts. One problem with this method is that the joists must be offset to overlap on interior girts if there are several spans of joists. If 4 × 8 sheets of plywood are being used, this may cause problems with the subflooring, since the sheets must be adjusted and cut to line up with the spacing of the different joist spans.

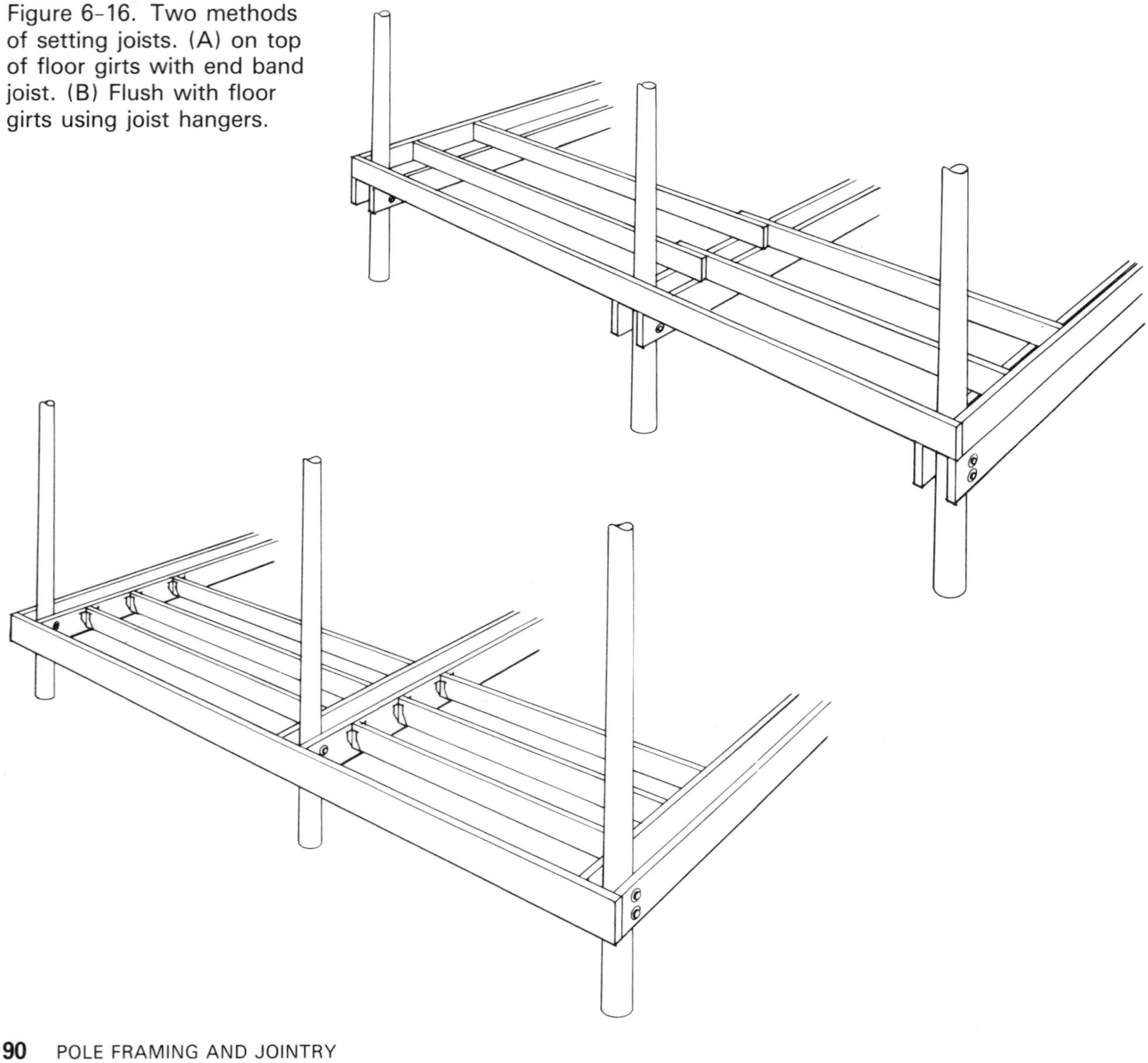

Figure 6-16. Two methods of setting joists. (A) on top of floor girts with end band joist. (B) Flush with floor girts using joist hangers.

By using joist hangers, the joists can all be set at the same spacing from the outside wall, eliminating any extra work with the subflooring. The girts also serve as the joist headers helping to cut material costs. Using joist hangers also conserves vertical space, since the joists are flush with the top of the girts. This may be an important consideration in a multi-floor building where several feet can be shaved off the height if the joists do not have to rest on top of the floor girts.

The normal rules of framing apply to floor framing in pole building. The joists around floor openings and under partitions should be doubled as shown in figure 6-17. Center cross bracing, widely used in the past, is unnecessary for most floor systems, due to the rigidity of modern plywood subflooring, which is glued and nailed in place.

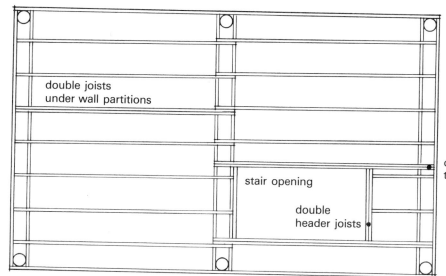

double joists
under wall partitions

stair opening

double
header joists

double
trimmer joists

Figure 6-17. Joists are normally framed 16 inches on center and doubled around stair openings and under walls.

Subfloor Decking

The subfloor is normally installed immediately after framing to provide a good working platform as construction continues. Subflooring can be ¾-inch tongue-and-groove plywood that will be covered later with wood flooring, carpet, vinyl flooring, or simply left as is for a shop floor. Plywood subflooring is much stronger and won't develop squeaks, if construction adhesive is applied to the joists as it is being nailed down. The adhesive is applied with a large caulking gun on one area at a time as the panels are set in place.

One-by-six spruce boards can also be used as subflooring but installation is much more labor intensive than plywood. Unless you can get the boards at a real savings, it will pay to use plywood.

Tongue-and-groove 2 × 6 planks can be used for flooring without putting down any subflooring. Two-by-six planks set on top of joists, spaced 16 inches on center (o.c.), form a rugged and economical floor. It is important that such planks be tongue-and-

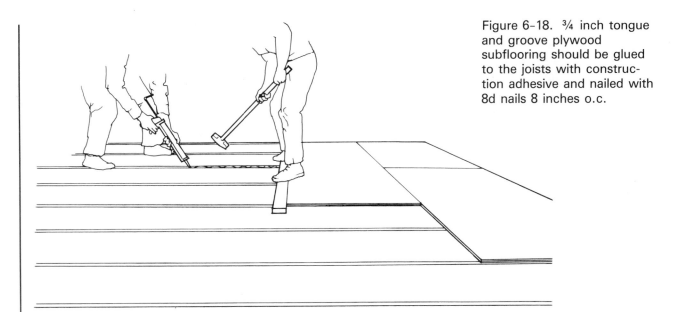

Figure 6-18. ¾ inch tongue and groove plywood subflooring should be glued to the joists with construction adhesive and nailed with 8d nails 8 inches o.c.

groove to form an airtight platform over crawl spaces. These planks must be extremely dry to avoid shrinkage and warping after they are laid in place.

Wall Framing

Wall framing in pole construction can take many forms depending on the function of the walls. Since the exterior walls in pole buildings are non-loadbearing, they are used for framing doors and windows, as a nail base for the siding or interior wall covering, and for holding insulation. The complexity of the wall frame will depend on how many of these tasks it must do.

The simplest wall system might be found in a pole barn where framing is only necessary to carry the siding and to frame a few doors and windows. Figure 6–19 illustrates such a case where 2×4 siding girts are used as a nail base for board and batten siding. A simple 2×4 box frame is built to carry the doors and windows.

If the barn were to be insulated and finished on the inside, then additional framing is needed for an inside nailbase and to hold the insulation. Figure 6–19 shows one way to do this using 2×4 bracing, nailed to the back of the siding girts. Four inches of fiberglass insulation can be laid horizontally between the 2×4 braces and interior board or plywood sheathing can be nailed to the 2×4s. To get a thicker wall for more insulation, 2×6 bracing could also be used. Because the siding girts are plumb, the interior wall will also be plumb with the wall boards simply butting against the poles.

The foundation poles of a pole building are often left outside the building, so that stud walls can be built inside of them. This saves the labor expense of working the siding around irregular poles. In this case, the walls are framed as in conventional platform

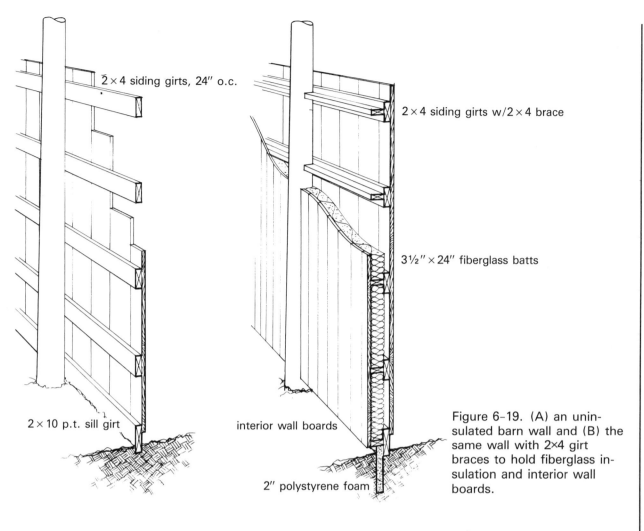

2 × 4 siding girts, 24″ o.c.

2 × 4 siding girts w/2 × 4 brace

3½″ × 24″ fiberglass batts

2 × 10 p.t. sill girt

interior wall boards

2″ polystyrene foam

Figure 6–19. (A) an unin-sulated barn wall and (B) the same wall with 2×4 girt braces to hold fiberglass in-sulation and interior wall boards.

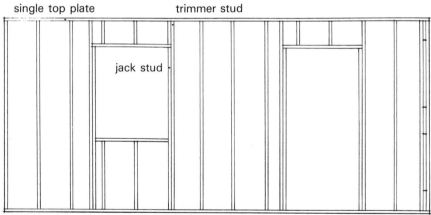

single top plate   trimmer stud

jack stud

Figure 6–20. Stud wall fram-ing for pole buildings is simi-lar to conventional stud framing except there are no window or door headers or double top plate since the wall is non-loadbearing.

framing but with one big difference—there are no loadbearing headers over windows and doors. Figure 6–20 illustrates such a typ-ical wall. It uses 2 × 6s 24 inches on center (o.c.) so 6-inch fiberglass batts can be used. Notice that all that is necessary is a single top plate and a single piece of 2 × 6 over doors and windows, since there are no loads on the wall.

Framing a Stud Wall

Framing a stud wall, pole style, is slightly different than in conventional construction. First, there are no load-carrying headers, only top and bottom plates to frame-out doors and windows. Secondly, stud spacing should always be 24 inches on center (o.c.) regardless of whether you are using 2×4s, 2×6s, or 2×8s. This spacing is not required because of any load but as a nail base for sheathing and siding and to hold fiberglass batt insulation.

Normally, stud walls are built on the ground and then tipped up into place. This is how it should be done in pole construction, but you might run into a small problem if the walls are built after all the floors are in place. Basically, an 8-foot wall will not tip up into an 8-foot high space; it will catch on the ceiling joists. The solution is to frame it ½-inch shorter and then shim it to the joists with plywood shims and shim shingles, once it is upright. Of course, you can build the wall in place and toenail each stud into the top and bottom plates, but this will usually take much longer than the shim method.

Start by laying out the top and bottom wall plate with lines indicating the position of the studs 24 inches on center (o.c.) and the window, door studs, and jacks. Cut the two plates to length and lay them on the floor side by side. Starting from the end of the plate, make marks ¾-inch on either side of every 2-foot interval. Use a pocket square to mark these lines across both plates and put an X in the middle of them to mark that it is the location of a stud. Put a stud mark every 2 feet even if it is under a window or in a door opening. You will want to have a nailer there to catch the sheathing around the opening.

Next, mark the location of the rough opening for your doors and windows. The rough opening dimensions are available from the distributors of pre-made units or can be figured by adding 2½ inches onto the width and height of site made units. Because doors and windows should have a double stud on either side for stiffness, mark out the rough opening, add a jack stud on either side and then a full stud outside of the jack studs. Put a J between the lines for the jack studs to remind you that these will only run to the top of the window or door. Any 24-inch on center (o.c.) studs that fall in a window or door opening need to be marked with a C for cripple stud. Cripple studs are short studs that run from the top or bottom plate to the door or window opening.

You can now cut all your studs, cripples, and jacks to the proper height (taking into account the top and bottom plate) and nail them in place between the two plates. Use two 10d nails driven through the top and bottom plate to secure each stud. The jack studs should be nailed into the studs next to them. Then cut the plates for the windows and doors and nail these on top of the jack studs and between them for the bottoms of windows. Finally, nail in place any cripple studs around windows or doors.

The wall is now ready to stand up into place and nail to the floor and ceiling framing. Use ½-inch plywood shims and shim shingles to get a tight fit against the ceiling joists if you had to shorten the wall to get it upright.

Superinsulated Walls

Because the walls in a pole building are non-loadbearing, this offers great opportunities for using superinsulation techniques that can dramatically cut heating bills in cold northern climates. Most superinsulation techniques rely on a very thick wall that can hold lots of insulation. In a pole building, this can be done very easily by using two 2 × 4 walls that are spaced apart and filled with insulation between them. Figure 6–21 shows such a design where both walls are framed with 2 × 4s 24 inches on center (o.c.) and separated by a 5-inch air space so the total wall thickness is 12 inches.

- The vapor barrier would go on the outside of the inside wall so wiring and plumbing could be run in the wall without penetrating it, eliminating air infiltration and moisture problems.
- The outer 2 × 4 wall and the space between the two walls would be filled with 8½ inches of fiberglass, so there is a complete insulation barrier and no thermal bridges across the wall.
- The inner wall would be filled with 3½ inches of fiberglass, giving a total R value for the entire wall system of over 40!

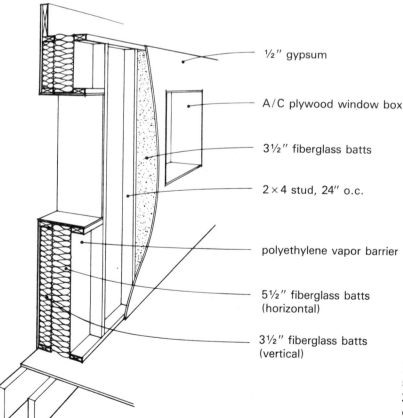

½″ gypsum

A/C plywood window box

3½″ fiberglass batts

2 × 4 stud, 24″ o.c.

polyethylene vapor barrier

5½″ fiberglass batts (horizontal)

3½″ fiberglass batts (vertical)

Figure 6–21. A superinsulated wall detail using two 2×4 walls with a total R-value of 40.

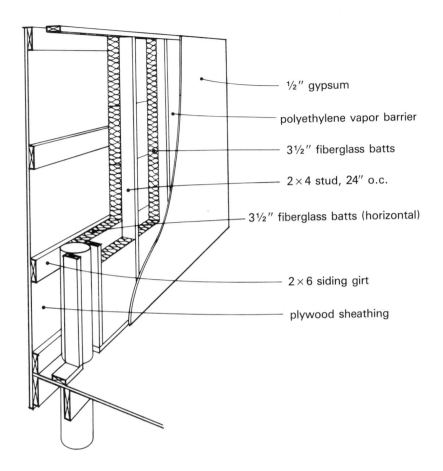

Figure 6-22. The wall framing detail of the Pole Cabin from Part 2 which uses an inner 2×4 wall to create two insulation cavities.

½″ gypsum

polyethylene vapor barrier

3½″ fiberglass batts

2 × 4 stud, 24″ o.c.

3½″ fiberglass batts (horizontal)

2 × 6 siding girt

plywood sheathing

The pole cabin that is detailed in Part 2 has even a simpler superinsulated wall. The siding is hung on exterior girts on the north and east walls and then a 2 × 4 wall is built inside the poles. This makes a 8-inch cavity for insulation between the inside face of the 2 × 4 and the exterior siding.

Laminated panels. Laminated panels of plywood and foam, often called *stress-skin panels* are revolutionizing post and beam and pole building techniques. These panels come in 4 × 8 or longer lengths and can be custom-made with different thicknesses of foam insulation and different coverings.

A popular panel consists of ½-inch exterior plywood siding, 5½ inches of foam, and ½-inch drywall on the inside. It can be put directly onto posts or girts with long pole spikes, and cuts framing and finish costs dramatically. In 3 or 4 days a house can be framed with the siding and drywall in place!

Framing techniques vary for different kinds of panels, but figure 6–23 shows how one pole house was built using stress-skined panels for the floors, walls, and roof. Ten-foot wall panels were nailed directly onto the girts, flooring panels laid on top of the joists, and roof panels laid on the rafters. All the panels had an R-value of 38, making an airtight, superinsulated home. The envelope is so tight, in fact, that the owners must open a window slightly in order for their kitchen fan to draw.

Figure 6-23. Stressed-skin panels with up to 5½" thick foam cores can be used for siding, flooring, and roofing to form a superinsulated house envelope with a minimum of framing.

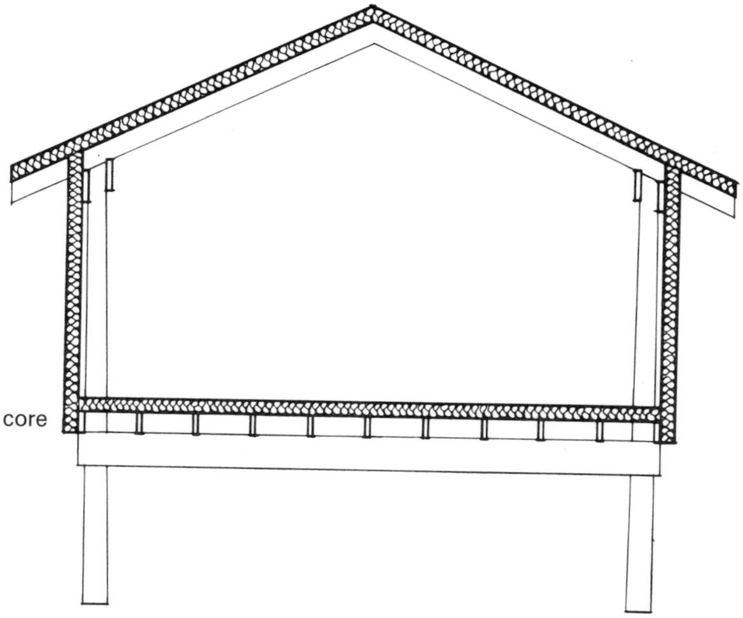

4 × 10 stressed-skin panels with 5½" foam insulating core

Using Green Lumber

Using rough-sawn, native lumber that comes directly from the mill or is milled right on site, is an excellent way to save money on materials. Undimensioned and undried lumber, often known as green lumber, is usually two-thirds the cost of kiln-dried lumber and is available in all parts of the country. Despite its cost advantages, it is harder to work with because it is wet and heavy and has uneven dimensions.

Using Shims

Rough 2× stock can be used for floor and wall framing despite its uneven dimensions. Rough lumber often has variations in width up to ¼-inch which can play havoc with the surface of a wall or floor, unless you take precautions.

For wall framing, make sure to line up the studs with the inside of the wall, letting the other side vary. You can then use 1 × 3 horizontal strapping and shims on the outside to get an even nailing base. Often it is unnecessary to shim the strapping if there is only a small variation from stud to stud.

For floor framing, it is necessary to sort the joists, and pick the two widest pieces to be used as the outside band joists. The two end joists are then set in place with a string stretched over the top between them. Then the other joists, whose widths are equal to or less than the outer ones, are set in place. The inner joists can simply be raised up with a shim shingle driven under them until they touch the string. The tops of all the joists will now be flush for the subflooring.

When using rough cut lumber for rafter framing, the same

method of using the widest pieces on the outside and shimming the middle rafters should be followed. This will give an even surface for the roof deck. The underside of the rafters can be evened out with strapping, if necessary, for finishing them as an exposed cathedral ceiling.

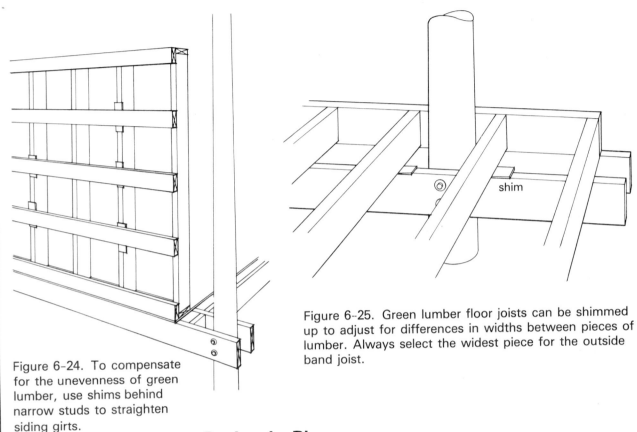

Figure 6-24. To compensate for the unevenness of green lumber, use shims behind narrow studs to straighten siding girts.

Figure 6-25. Green lumber floor joists can be shimmed up to adjust for differences in widths between pieces of lumber. Always select the widest piece for the outside band joist.

Drying in Place

Because green lumber is often 50 percent water by weight, walls, floors, and roofs framed with green lumber should never be tightly enclosed with a vapor barrier and drywall immediately after framing. It is fine to insulate walls and floors, but leave the interior surface open so that the moisture can escape from the wood. Three to six months is usually necessary for the wood to give up most of its moisture and reach equilibrium with the surrounding air.

Green lumber should always be fastened with galvanized nails so that the nails will not rust. They also will hold better after the wood has dried and shrunk.

Temporary Supports

Because of its moisture, green lumber can be somewhat weaker when it is fresh off the stump than its kiln-dried counterpart. After it has dried, however, it is considerably stronger due to its larger dimensions (a rough cut 2 × 6 has 45 percent more wood in it than a kiln-dried 2×6 that actually measures $5\frac{1}{2} \times 1\frac{1}{2}$ inches). The initial weakness of green lumber should be taken into account when sizing green wood beams that will carry concentrated loads. A temporary center support for a beam will keep it from sagging and can be removed in 6 months, when the beam has dried out.

Sealing Pressure-treated Poles

Because of the toxic preservatives in pressure-treated poles, they should be effectively sealed off or covered if there is any possibility of human or animal contamination.

For livestock barns, where poles are in the walls and covered by the siding on the outside but left uncovered on the inside, they should be boxed. You can use rough 1×8 boards to box the poles to a height of 8 feet. This will prevent animals from rubbing against or chewing on the poles.

In tightly sealed houses, where the poles are in the wall, they should be painted with a varnish or shellac before they are enclosed in the wall. This will prevent any toxic odors from building up in the wall and getting into the house. For poles that are on the interior of a house, they should be painted with several coats of varnish. They may then be boxed with pine or Sheetrock to conceal them or left exposed.

ROOFING AND SIDING

CHAPTER SEVEN

The material choices for roofing and siding depend on three main factors: cost, durability, and aesthetics. The durability of roofing and siding is usually proportional to cost. Therefore, the economic life of the building should be considered when choosing these materials. An expensive terne metal roof, for example, that might last 100 years, would be a very poor investment on a farm building that might only be used for 30 years.

The choice of roofing and siding is also very much an aesthetic question. What would look right, given the building, its shape, and the surrounding environment? The best way to make this choice is to do some sightseeing. Look at other buildings in your area, see what the predominant materials are, and see what appeals to you. Remember that the siding and roofing will determine in large part what your pole building looks like, whether it appears conventional or unusual, modern or rustic. Once you have found materials that appeal to you, then you must reconcile your taste with your building budget.

Roofing

There are many different types of roofing products made from metal, wood, fiberglass, asphalt, and other materials. Table 7–1 lists various roofing materials and ranks them in terms of expense, durability and special characteristics.

Roof Decking and Trim

The first step in roofing is to put down a deck or nailing base for the roofing material. Different materials and rafter layouts require different types of decking.

For *fiberglass shingles* and *asphalt roll roofing*, a solid deck of ½-inch plywood or chipboard is usually used, but 1× spruce boards can also be used. However, the material cost is about the same and the labor much greater than when using 4 × 8 panels. When installing the decking, make sure it overhangs the bottom of the rafters and the rake rafters by enough to cover the fascia boards, usually ¾-inch.

For *metal roofing*, 1 × 3 strapping is usually used, spaced 24 inches on center (o.c.). This means less labor and material costs for most types of metal roofing and is one of its main advantages. Always check the roofing manufacturer's recommendation for decking first, since improper support may invalidate any warranty on the roofing.

Cathedral ceilings. On rafter and purlin framing, with large rafters spaced 4 to 8 feet apart, 2 × 6 tongue-and-groove planks can be used for decking. This provides a solid roof deck and also an attractive interior finish for cathedral ceilings where the rafter beams are left exposed. For exposed cathedral ceilings, foam insulation is applied over the decking and then covered with the roofing material. Foam-filled stress-skin panels may also be used in the same manner for insulated roof decking.

After the roof deck is on, the fascia trim boards must be installed so the metal drip edge can be put on over them. Fascia boards are usually 1× stock nailed directly onto the tail cuts of the rafters with 8d galvanized box nails. Fascia boards also cover the rake rafters on the gable ends and should be butted up tight under the roof deck.

Galvanized metal drip edge is then fastened to the roof edges with roofing nails. The drip edge forms a straight edge for lining up the finish roof, giving a neater appearance. It also keeps water from dripping on and discoloring the fascia boards.

After the drip edge is on, 15 lb. roofing felt, commonly known

Siding and roofing are two of the most important factors in the appearance of a building. Here vertical board siding is applied to the Wolff house in northern Vermont.

Table 7-1

COMPARISON OF ROOFING MATERIALS

Type	Weight[1]	Durability[2]	Cost[3]
Asphalt half lap	90	low	low
Fiberglass shingles	235	low-med	low
Asphalt/Plastic membrane		med	med
Cedar shingles (18″)	158	med-high	med
Galvanized steel	113	low-med	low
Galvanized steel, prepainted	113	med	med
Terne metal	90	high	high
Cor-ten steel	270	med-high	med
Slate	700	high	high

1. Weight is in lbs./SQ. (100 sq. ft.) installed
2. Approximate durability scale: low = 15 years, med. = 20-30 years, high = 40 years or longer
3. Approximate cost scale (1985): low = $1/sq. ft. installed, med. = $3/sq. ft., high = $5/sq. ft.

as tar paper, is put over the decking to protect it until the finished roofing is installed. This should be overlapped a minimum of 4 inches to form a watertight seal and stapled to the roof decking.

Metal Roofing

Metal roofing comes in a wide variety of materials, coatings, and sizes. Because of its durability, ease of installation, and the fact that 1 × 3 nailers are all that is necessary for decking, it is often the most economical choice for roofing.

Corrugated galvanized steel is the most common metal roofing material, in part because it is the least expensive. The metal sheets are dipped in a zinc or zinc/aluminum finish that protects the metal from rusting. The zinc coating, however, eventually wears away and the roofing will begin to rust. A protective coat of paint, touched up every five years, will help slow down the erosion of the zinc plating and greatly prolong the life of the roofing. Twenty-six gauge (.022 in.) steel is standard for galvanized steel roofing and can safely span strapping placed 24 inches on center (o.c.). It should contain at least 1.25 oz. of zinc per sq. ft.; sheets with less zinc will corrode very rapidly.

Terne metal roofing is another steel product that is coated

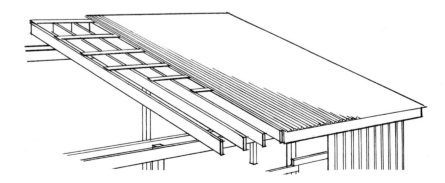

Figure 7-1. Galvanized metal roofing detail.

A standing-seam terne metal roof is both attractive and durable.

with a mixture of lead and tin. This type of roofing has been used since the 1800s and is more durable than steel with the zinc coating. It comes in flat sheets with an edge seam that crimps over the adjoining sheet. It is usually installed by professional roofers who have the proper crimping tools. It also must be primed and painted.

Cor-ten is a weathering steel made by U.S. Steel that includes small amounts of chromium, copper, nickel, and other elements to resist deep rusting. Its surface, however, does rust to a deep red color and this oxidation provides the protection against deeper rusting. Eighteen gauge (.048 in.) is a standard weight for this roofing, making it twice as thick as regular galvanized roofing. While it is much more durable, it is almost twice as expensive as galvanized roofing.

Aluminum is also used for roofing, and though it tends to be softer and weaker than galvanized steel, it resists corrosion in salt environments much better. Thus aluminum is a good choice in coastal areas. Aluminum is highly reactive with other metals so aluminum or stainless steel nails must be used to fasten it.

Fiberglass and Asphalt Roofing

Asphalt or the newer fiberglass shingles are the most common roofing material for residential construction. They require a solid roof deck and a moderate amount of labor to install, but they are inexpensive and last 20 years or longer. They are also available in a wide range of colors and styles to suit almost any taste.

The standard shingles for residential construction are 235 lb. fiberglass shingles (they weigh 235 lbs. per 100 square feet). They come in bundles that cover 33⅓ sq. ft., but are ordered by the square (100 square feet). Most carry limited warranties of up to 20 years. Shingles can be used on roofs with slopes over 3 in 12.

For lower pitched roofs, you must use asphalt half-lap roll roofing. This comes in a continuous roll that covers 50 sq. ft. Half the surface is smooth, the other half covered with mineral granules like asphalt shingles. The roofing is laid in horizontal rows, overlapping sheets by half their width and sealing them with a tar substance called *blind nailing cement*. This forms a water-tight surface that has the same characteristics as asphalt shingles and looks somewhat similar. Care should be taken to always roll out and warm up

Installing Roof Decking

Using ½-inch plywood or chipboard is a quick and efficient way to deck a roof. Set up two ladders next to each other so the 4 × 8 sheets can be carried up to roof height by two people.

First, take a measurement from the outside of the rake rafter to the rafter that is 6 feet on center (o.c.) from the building's edge. Cut the first sheet of decking so that it overhangs the rake rafter by ¾-inch to cover the fascia boards, and lands halfway on the inside rafter. This sheet can be nailed in place with 8d nails every 8 inches working off the ladders. Make sure the bottom of the sheet overhangs the ends of the rafters by ¾-inch to cover the eave fascia. The rest of the sheets for the first row can be put on without cutting since there is a rafter every 8 feet on center (o.c.). Cut the last piece so it overhangs the rake rafter on the other end by ¾-inch.

One common problem often encountered in roof decking is that the rafters are not quite square to the building's walls. This causes the decking to run off the rake rafter and its end nailing rafter when the piece is lined up to evenly overhang the tail cuts. Having a good nailer at the joints is what's critical (since you only have ¾-inch to play with), so position the sheets so they land evenly on the rafters. The bottom overhang will now begin to run off, but this can later be trimmed back with a circular saw. Make sure you determine which way the decking is running off, so that there is at least ¾-inch overhang along the entire eave.

The second row of decking should overlap the joints on the first row so the joints do not fall all on the same rafters. Start the second row halfway on the second rafter in from the edge of the building and then cut a short piece to span from

it out over the rake rafter. Alternate this pattern of rows as you work up to the peak of the roof. If the deck is too steep to stand on, then you can use 2 × 4 cleats nailed into the decking and rafters to give you a foothold as you work your way up.

The last row of decking must be ripped down to the proper width so it extends just to the peak. If there is going to be a ridge vent for roof ventilation, cut the plywood back a little further to leave a 1-inch gap between it and the ridge board.

The ¾-inch overhang on the edges of the deck should now be checked. If the decking runs off, snap a chalk line to mark the proper overhang and cut the decking back with a circular saw.

The roof deck should now be covered with tar paper to protect it from the rain. If you had to use 2 × 4 cleats to stand on, install the tar paper from top down, leaving the bottom edge unstapled so you can slip the next row down under its edge to form a waterproof seal. That way you don't have to pull the cleats off and nail them on again as you work back up. If you have a low-sloped roof that you can stand on without cleats, then it makes sense to install the tar paper in the conventional manner, from bottom up, lapping the rows as you go.

Before the finished roofing can go on, the fascia boards and galvanized drip edge must be installed. The fascia boards are simply butted up under the plywood decking and attached to the tail cut on the eave rafters and the side of the rake rafter with 8d galvanized box nails. The drip edge is then nailed onto the edges of the roof on top of the tar paper with 1¼-inch roofing nails driven along its back edge.

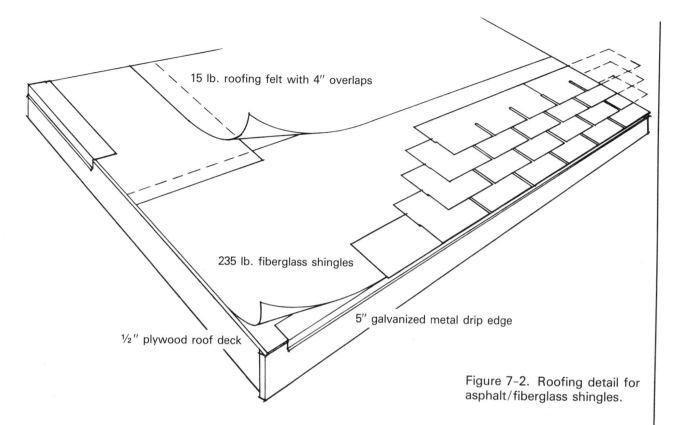

15 lb. roofing felt with 4″ overlaps

235 lb. fiberglass shingles

5″ galvanized metal drip edge

½″ plywood roof deck

Figure 7-2. Roofing detail for asphalt/fiberglass shingles.

the roll roofing before it is put in place. Otherwise it will expand after it has been nailed, causing bubbles and waves that are unsightly as well as potential areas for leaks.

Built-up tar roofing is also used on flat and low sloped roofs. It consists of layers of roofing felt and hot tar built up in place. Normally, 5 to 7 layers of felt and tar are used. Recently, special rubber and plastic membranes have begun to replace built-up tar roofing as a way to seal flat roofs. These new membranes are more expensive than the old-fashioned hot tar method, but are much more durable and cost-effective in the long run.

Soffits and Roof Ventilation

The eaves of a building, where the roof overhangs the wall, should always be closed off to keep out animals, insects, and the weather. At the same time, it is necessary to ventilate most attic areas to remove moisture that accumulates under the roof. Ventilation is also important to help keep the attic cool in the summer, and to keep the roof surface cold in winter which prevents ice build-up along the eaves.

The most satisfactory way to ventilate roof areas is with soffit and ridge vents. A continuous strip of screened vent is located in the middle of the soffit and another continuous screened vent is put at the peak of the roof. This allows air to enter the bottom of the roof, flow under the rafters, and exit at the top. Pre-made aluminum soffit and ridge vents are available from most building suppliers.

Another method is to put vents near the peak on the gable ends of the building. This does allow for ventilation of an attic area, but it doesn't ventilate the entire roof surface as soffit vents do. Figure 7–3 shows these two different methods of roof ventilation.

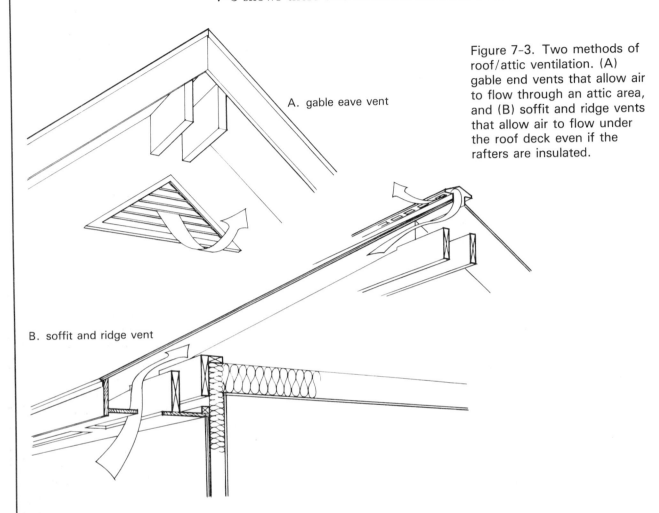

A. gable eave vent

B. soffit and ridge vent

Figure 7–3. Two methods of roof/attic ventilation. (A) gable end vents that allow air to flow through an attic area, and (B) soffit and ridge vents that allow air to flow under the roof deck even if the rafters are insulated.

Installing Soffits and Returns

Soffit boards can be made from either ½-inch A/C plywood or 1× pine boards. On a sloping soffit detail, the soffit is simply nailed to the underside of the rafters. On a horizontal soffit detail, both the eave and rake soffits are nailed to the 2 × 4 lookouts that extend out from the building to the fascia board. Use 6d galvanized box nails to secure the soffit. If a standard 2-inch vent strip is used along the eave soffits, the strip is nailed in place first and then 2 soffit boards fitted on either side of it.

On buildings with a horizontal soffit detail, because the eave soffit and the rake soffit do not meet on the same plane, there needs to be some special trim work where they meet. This piece of trim is called a *return* and can either be a simple triangular piece of wood that joins the 2 soffits or a more elaborate and ornate framed return that is actually a miniature roof. Figure 7–4 shows a simple return detail that is a triangular block that attaches to the end of

Installing Shingles

To install asphalt or fiberglass shingles you will need the following tools: a hammer, a utility knife, a rafter square, and a small trowel for the roof cement. If the roof pitch is too steep to stand on, you will need a set of *roofing jacks* to hold staging boards as you work up the roof. Jacks are wooden brackets with a special metal head flange that can be nailed under a completed row of shingles so that you do not damage the finished roof. You will also need 1¼-inch galvanized roofing nails and a gallon of plastic roofing cement to seal the shingles along the roof edge and valleys.

Follow the manufacturer's directions for installation that are on the shingle packages. Various styles of shingles have small differences in installation, but these are the basic steps:

1. **Install the starter course.** The starter course is a strip of shingles that are cut in half width-wise and installed with their bottoms facing the peak of the roof and their tar tabs on the bottom running along the drip edge. This strip is necessary to cover under the tab cutouts of the first full row of shingles. It also anchors the lower edge that runs along the eaves.

2. **Cut three different lengths of starter shingles.** Starter shingles are the ones that will go along the rake edge of the roof as you move upward. You should cut full length shingles (with just the ear removed so you have a straight line at the roof edge), a ⅔-length shingle, and a ⅓-length shingle. Alternate these starter shingles as you put on successive rows to prevent the end seams between the shingles from lining up and forming a potential leak area.

3. **Begin with a full length starter for the first row.** Put a bead of plastic cement on the rake drip edge and nail the shingle over the starter course. Use four nails per shingle, driven at the height of the tar tabs so they will be covered by the next row. Put two more shingles on this row, and then start the second row with a ⅔-length shingle. Line up the ears on the shingle so they sit on the top of the first row. This will give you about a 5 to 5½-inch exposure on each of the rows of shingles. Put two more full shingles on the second row, and then start the third row with a ⅓-length shingle.

4. **Finish these first three rows across the entire roof.** If you have a steep roof, roofing jacks can now be set on top of the third row to hold 2 × 10 staging. Jacks should be set 4 feet on center (o.c.) with galvanized nails driven into the roof rafters. When you have the staging set up, you can haul bundles of shingles up onto the roof and do your cutting on the staging so you don't have to keep going up and down a ladder.

5. **Finish off the rest of the rows using alternating starter lengths and making sure to cement the shingles along both rake edges.** Keep setting rows of jacks as necessary to move up the roof. Normally, rows of jacks are set about 4 feet apart so it is easy to move up and down them without damaging the roof surface.

6. **On gable roofs, after both sides are shingled, a special cap row is put over the ridge if there is no ridge vent.** This cap row consists of ⅓-length shingles with the top edges trimmed back at a slight angle. Starting at the side of the house which is away from the prevailing winds, the shingles are bent over the peak sideways and nailed in place. The next cap shingle overlaps the first, leaving 5 inches exposed. Continue overlapping the shingles in this manner until the entire ridge is capped. The top of the final cap shingle should be cut off so only the mineral surface is left. Cement and nail this in place, and the roof is finished.

the eave soffit, extending up to meet the rake soffit. A vertical piece then closes off the back of the triangle.

On pole buildings where the rafter girts extend out beyond the building's wall to carry the end rake rafters, the return must be framed around the rafter girts. Figure 7–5 shows a return detail with a triangular piece that is nailed directly onto the end of the rafter girt. If you have a shallow roof slope and large rafter girts, the girt may stick down below the eave soffit so far that the return would have to be very large and awkward to completely cover it. The solution is to cut the rafter girt down to a narrower size where it extends from the building. Since it is only carrying the one rake rafter, a 2×12 can safely be trimmed down to a 2×6, so the eave soffit is flush with the bottom.

Figure 7-4. Eave return detail that joins the horizontal soffit with the sloping rake soffit.

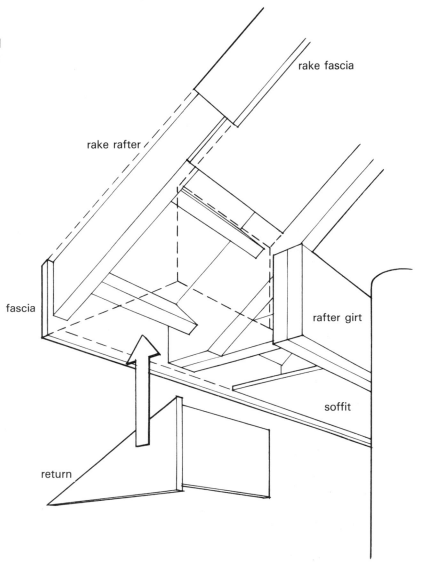

Siding

Siding materials are as numerous as roofing materials, and again a choice must be made on cost, durability and aesthetics. Table 7–2 compares the most common siding materials that are available. Table 7–3 lists the weathering characteristics of wood sidings.

Table 7-2

COMPARISON OF SIDING MATERIALS

Type	Dimensions		Sheathing Required?	Durability[1]	Cost[2]
	Width	Length			
Hardboard	12"	16'	yes	low	low
Board-and-batten	6" or 8"	8'	no	low-med	low
Shiplap boards	6" or 8"	8'	no	low-med	low
Plywood siding	4'	8'	no	low-med	low-med
Bevel siding	5" or 6"	2' to 6'	yes	high	high
Drop siding	6"	12' to 16'	no	high	med
Cedar shingles	random	16" to 24"	yes	high	high
Aluminum/Vinyl	12"	12'	yes	med	med

1. Durability based on weathering characteristics and resistance to puncture damage.
2. Approximate cost scale (1985): Low = $1/sq. ft. installed, med. = $2/sq. ft., high = $3/sq. ft.

Sheathing

The main function of sheathing is as a nail base for siding such as clapboards or shingles. It also serves as an air barrier, stopping air infiltration that gets past the siding. A final but important use of sheathing in conventional construction is to brace stud walls. A loadbearing stud wall must have diagonal bracing to keep it from racking under pressure. Half-inch plywood sheathing serves all these purposes very well.

In pole building, however, the siding is often carried by the girts, and bracing is not necessary because of the integral pole structure. This means that sheathing is unnecessary in many different methods of wall and siding construction. A well-designed pole house will minimize the use of sheathing, incorporating it only as necessary for air infiltration control or as a nail base on stud walls.

Half-inch plywood sheathing or chipboard is commonly used to cover stud walls. It goes on quickly, seals the wall, braces it, and is a good nail base for any type of siding. Pressboard sheathing such as Homosote is also used as an insulating nail base where rigidity for bracing is not important. Foam-backed sheathing panels that provide a nailing base with a high R-value are also manufactured. Their square foot cost, however, is high compared with fiberglass insulation.

Make sure you think about the necessity of sheathing in terms of a nail base, an air barrier, and bracing. Often you'll find that with pole construction, you can eliminate it, saving time and money.

There are many instances where sheathing is not necessary. If you are using plywood siding, it does the job of sealing and bracing all in one. If you are using vertical board siding over girts then no sheathing is necessary unless you are concerned about air infiltration. If that is the case, it would be wise to use an insulating com-

Table 7-3

WEATHERING CHARACTERISTICS OF WOOD

Softwoods	Resistance to Cupping 1 = Best 4 = Worst	Conspicuousness of Checking 1 = Least 2 = Most	Ease of Keeping Well Painted 1 = Easiest 4 = Hardest
Cedar, Alaska	1	1	1
Cedar, white	1	—	1
Redwood	1	1	1
Pine, eastern white	2	2	2
Pine, sugar	2	2	2
Hemlock	2	2	3
Spruce	2	2	3
Douglas fir	2	2	4
Hardwoods			
Beech	4	2	4
Birch	4	2	4
Maple	4	2	4
Ash	4	2	3
Chestnut	3	2	3
Walnut	3	2	3
Elm	4	2	4
Oak, white	4	2	4

(From: Wood Handbook, Agriculture Handbook No. 72, USDA.)

posite sheathing such as Homosote. If you are using drop siding which consists of tongue-and-groove boards, it can be nailed directly into the studs.

Air barriers. On insulated buildings, it makes sense to use a newly developed wrap called Tyvek. This is an air barrier made from spun olefin fibers that effectively cuts down infiltration while allowing moisture from the building to escape. Tyvek can be used over girt framing even when no sheathing is used to reduce air infiltration. Because polyethylene or tar paper will trap moisture in the walls, you should never use these as an air barrier on the outside of a house.

Figure 7-5. Five types of exterior sheathing.

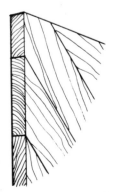 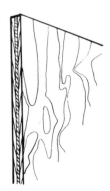 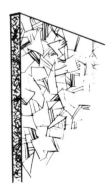 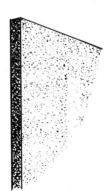 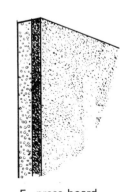

A. diagonal boards   B. ½″ plywood   C. chip board   D. press board nailbase   E. press board with foam backing

Green, rough-cut boards are an inexpensive and durable siding material. Shown here is vertical 1×6 shiplap pine.

Vertical Board Siding

Vertical boards are an attractive, durable, and extremely low-cost siding material. Not only can they go on directly over pole girts, saving the time and expense of sheathing, but you can also use inexpensive green lumber. These two advantages make vertical board siding one-third the cost of conventional wood clapboard siding when you take into account labor and materials.

Vertical boards can be put on in several styles to form a weathertight seal. *Board-and-batten* is a common style that uses 1 × 6 boards butted together and then a 1 × 2 batten over the seam. The batten seals the seam and hides the expansion and contraction of the siding boards. *Board-on-batten* is similar except the battens are behind the boards and the boards are usually gapped a half-inch or more to give a visually appealing relief. *Board-on-board* is yet another style where the boards are spaced wider apart and overlapped.

Vertical siding can be made weathertight without battens by using boards with a tongue-and-groove or shiplap edge. *V-groove* is a type of tongue-and-groove board that makes an attractive siding material. *Shiplap* boards simply have an edge that overlaps the adjacent board to form a tight seal.

While green lumber boards can be milled with a V-groove or

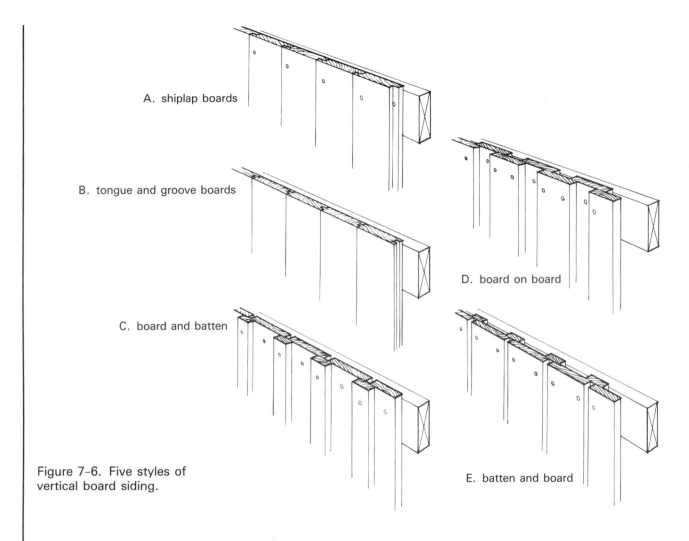

A. shiplap boards

B. tongue and groove boards

C. board and batten

D. board on board

E. batten and board

Figure 7-6. Five styles of vertical board siding.

shiplap edge, it is wise to air dry them for several months before installing, so that the shrinkage does not open up the joints. Board-and-batten siding can be installed dripping wet, since the battens can easily cover the ¼-inch shrinkage that normally occurs on a 1 × 6 board.

To install vertical board siding, there must be horizontal nailers every 2 feet. These can be either 2× pole girts or 1 × 3 strapping put on a stud wall. Boards are attached with 8d galvanized nails. Each board should be plumbed with a level to keep the seams running vertically. This is especially important with rough-sawn lumber that may vary in width from one end of the board to the other. For tall walls, siding boards may be joined by either cutting a 45 degree bevel cut and letting the top board overlap the bottom one, or by using a piece of metal flashing where the two boards butt together.

Panel Siding

Another economical kind of siding is *303 plywood siding* (see table 7–4). This comes in a wide variety of textures and can be ordered in redwood, cedar, southern yellow pine, Douglas fir, and other woods. Texture 1–11 is a standard style that has grooves 8 inches on center (o.c.) to simulate board-on-batten siding.

Plywood siding comes in 4 × 8 sheets in either ⅜-inch, ½-inch, or ⅝-inch thicknesses. It can be special ordered in longer lengths or joined vertically using pre-made metal flashing.

Plywood siding has the advantage of going on quickly, eliminating any need for sheathing, and forming a tight exterior skin. It can be painted or stained like regular wood siding.

Stress-skin panels made of plywood siding, a foam core, and interior drywall or plywood are also available. These can be attached with pole spikes into a top and bottom pole girt to form an instant wall—siding, insulation, and interior finish all in one.

Corrugated metal siding is another option that is often used on barns and commercial buildings. It is easy to install, durable, and easier to maintain than wood. It does dent easily, however, which is a drawback for its use on animal housing. Metal siding normally comes in sheets 32 inches wide and 8 feet long. It can be special ordered to any length in 1-inch increments.

Metal siding is installed just like metal roofing with ring shanked nails with neoprene washers. It can be cut using a circular saw with an abrasive metal cutting blade.

Metal siding is easy to install and requires little maintenance.

A. cedar shingles

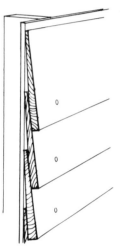

B. bevel siding

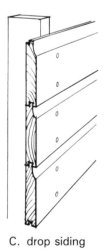

C. drop siding

Figure 7-7. Three types of traditional wood siding.

Traditional Wood Sidings

Bevel siding, shingles, and drop siding are three types of traditional wood siding that are installed horizontally. They are normally more expensive and require more labor to install than the sidings mentioned above. They are extremely durable, however, and are often chosen for residential construction for their aesthetic qualities.

Bevel siding is usually made out of spruce, cedar, or redwood and comes in widths ranging from 4 to 12 inches. It is installed over sheathing from bottom up, overlapping each piece to form a tight seal. Five and one-half inch bevel siding is a standard width that is overlapped so that 3 inches are left exposed on the piece below. This means that 1 board foot of siding will cover only ½-square foot of wall, an important point to remember when figuring costs and ordering. Bevel siding is nailed in place with 4d or 5d galvanized box nails driven about ½-inch from the lower edge.

Cedar shingles are tried and true siding material. They are durable and require no maintenance. Unpainted cedar will gradually weather to a dull brown if the shingles are cut from red cedar, or a silver-grey color if the shingles are white cedar. Shingles come in random widths and lengths or either 16,18, or 24 inches. They are overlapped by a half or more of their length; you should consult your building supplier to see how many square feet bundles sold locally will cover. Use 4d or 5d galvanized box nails for fastening the shingles, driven just above where the next higher shingle will cover, so there are no exposed nail heads.

Drop siding is made from boards, 1 × 6 or wider, with a tongue-and-groove joint. It is installed just like vertical V-groove siding except the boards run horizontally. This type of siding seems to have fallen out of style in the past several decades, despite its

Table 7-4

PLYWOOD SIDING

Type	Description
Rough-sawn	Rough surface without grooves
Texture 1-11	Rough-sawn, brushed, or coarse-sanded surface; 3/8″ grooves 4″ or 8″ on center
Kerf rough-sawn	Rough-sawn surface; narrow groves 4″ on center
Reverse board-and-batten	Rough-sawn, brushed, or coarse-sanded surface; 1-1/2″ grooves 12″ on center

Paint or Stain?

Wood siding should always be protected with a finish to prevent rapid weathering and discoloration. Even highly resistant cedar shingles will benefit from a coat of oil.

Paint has been the traditional finish for hundreds of years on wood buildings. Modern paints go on easily and protect very well, but it is an expensive finish to maintain. In areas with harsh climates, houses often should be repainted every four to five years. This means scraping, washing, priming, and repainting can often be the major expense in home maintenance.

A more economical alternative is to use a clear oil or oil stain. Oil stains come in a variety of natural wood colors and solid paint-like colors. It goes on very quickly and requires no preparation, such as the scraping and priming necessary for paint, when it is reapplied. Thus over the life of a building, stain will cost a fraction of what well maintained paint would cost.

For a clear finish on shingles or rough board siding, boiled linseed oil is excellent. Linseed oil is also non-toxic so it is a good choice for finishing livestock housing.

moderate cost and ease of installation. Because drop siding can be put on directly over studs without any exterior sheathing, its cost compares favorably with vertical siding and certainly requires a fraction of the labor that bevel siding or shingles do. As it becomes increasingly available in parts of the country, its popularity will probably rise again.

Foundation Skirts

To protect the underside of pole buildings from animals and the weather, it is often necessary to enclose the crawl space under the floor framing. In some designs with an elevated first floor, the underside of a pole house might be left open as a parking or storage area. Many pole buildings are built close to the ground, however, and it is an inconvenience as well as a hazard to have an open 12-inch space under the building.

Pressure-treated plywood. Pressure-treated plywood or a masonry parge treatment are two methods used to close off crawl spaces. Foam insulation can be put behind these skirts to insulate the crawl space and allow the natural warmth of the earth to serve as a buffer against heat loss from the ground floor.

Half-inch pressure-treated plywood is an easy way to install a long lasting skirt. The plywood can be attached to the poles, pole girts, or pressure-treated 2 × 4s that extend down from the floor framing. It is cut wide enough to extend from the bottom of the siding into the earth for several inches.

The plywood can be painted any color, such as a gray to simu-

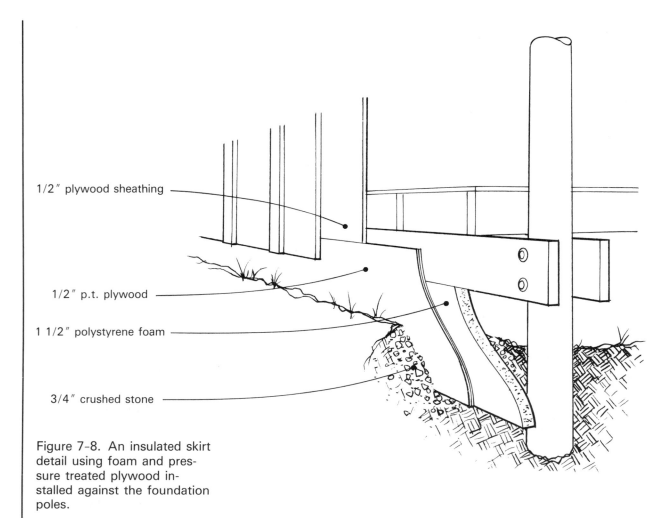

1/2″ plywood sheathing

1/2″ p.t. plywood

1 1/2″ polystyrene foam

3/4″ crushed stone

Figure 7-8. An insulated skirt detail using foam and pressure treated plywood installed against the foundation poles.

late the look of concrete, or a color to match the siding. Where the plywood is embedded in the ground, it should be backfilled with sand or gravel that won't soak up moisture, and thus expand when frozen.

Masonry parge. A parge of mortar with chopped fiberglass applied over wire mesh is another method of making a skirt. The special mortar is sold under several brand names and is used for surface bonding of concrete block. Make sure the mortar has chopped fiberglass strands in it; otherwise, the thin mortar coat will crack with the slightest movement in the skirt.

The mortar mixture is applied on a wire mesh or lath that is fastened to pressure-treated framing behind it. The lath should run from the bottom of the siding to several inches in the ground, similar to the plywood skirt. Usually two coats of mortar are applied, and the resulting finish looks remarkably like a concrete or masonry foundation.

In colder climates, it makes sense to put 2-inch polystyrene foundation insulation behind the skirts. When using plywood skirts, it can be glued with foam adhesive directly to the back of the plywood. On the mortar parge skirt, the lath and the insulation can be nailed together into the foundation framing. Polystyrene foam must be covered from sunlight to keep it from photodegrading. It is fine to leave it unprotected below grade.

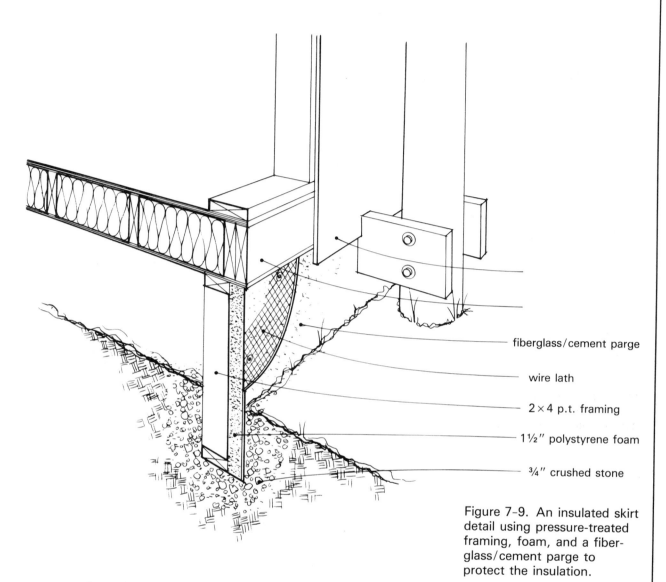

fiberglass/cement parge

wire lath

2 × 4 p.t. framing

1½″ polystyrene foam

¾″ crushed stone

Figure 7-9. An insulated skirt detail using pressure-treated framing, foam, and a fiberglass/cement parge to protect the insulation.

Foundation Vents. When a crawl space is closed off, it is important to take measures to reduce moisture and adequately ventilate it. To provide good cross ventilation, 8 × 12 operable foundation vents can be mounted in the plywood or parge skirt. In the winter, the vents can be closed to keep out infiltration. A 6 mil polyethylene vapor barrier on the ground in the crawl space is also a good idea to keep the earth's moisture from constantly moving up into the crawl space. These two precautions will ensure that your crawl space will remain free of moisture and fungus which could damage the building's framing.

Windows and Doors

CHAPTER EIGHT

The selection and placement of windows and doors is critical to the proper functioning of any building. Windows and doors control the natural light, ventilation, traffic patterns, and energy efficiency of a building. Window and door units also consume a large part of the construction budget, both for the cost of the units and the labor to install them. Careful planning and consideration before construction of window and door functions will result in an economical and efficient building design.

Windows

Windows can serve several functions in a building.

- Every type of window lets in natural daylight to illuminate the interior and decrease the need for artifical lighting.
- Operable windows with moveable sashes also can provide needed ventilation.
- Windows with clear glass provide a view to the outdoors. This serves the specific architectural function of integrating the interior with the outside environment, making the building seem larger and less claustrophobic.
- Finally, windows can also be a source of passive solar heat during the day and, of course, heat loss at night.

It is important to consider these functions in the planning stage, as you specify the types of windows you are going to use. For example, not every window in a house needs to be operable for ventilation. By plannning to use only a limited number of operable windows and making all the rest fixed glass, you can cut your window budget substantially, while making the house more energy-efficient. In a similar manner, by putting your large windows on the south wall of the house and few or none on the north wall, you can increase the natural daylight and passive solar heat entering the house.

Types of Windows

The basic parts of a window are the sash, jamb, and sill. The *sash* is the wooden frame that holds the glass. The sash is held by

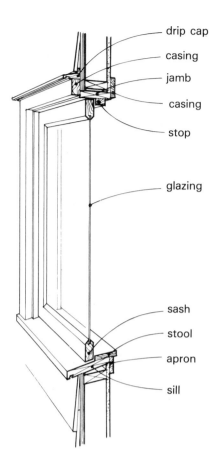

drip cap

casing

jamb

casing

stop

glazing

sash

stool

apron

sill

Figure 8-1. The parts of a window.

the *jambs* on the sides and top, and rests on the *sill* on the bottom. There are many different types of sash and jamb arrangements that have particular uses and advantages.

The *double hung window* is perhaps the most common, with two pieces of sash that slide up and down against the side jambs. Double hungs are widely used in residential construction because of their versatility and moderate cost. Their main disadvantage is a higher air infiltration rate as compared to casement or awning windows which have a single piece of sash. In general, a double hung window will have three times the air infiltration of a comparable casement or awning window.

Casement windows have a single piece of sash that is hinged on the side and swings out. This type of window is generally narrower than a double hung and is suited for applications which emphasize this vertical element. Because it has a tighter seal than a double hung window, it is more energy-efficient, but it usually costs more as well.

Awning windows are like casements except they are hinged on the top and open out and up. They are often used above kitchen sinks, in bathrooms, and other areas where there isn't enough wall height to install a tall window. They are similar in air tightness to casements.

Horizontal sliding windows are another option where wall height is limited. Most of these windows have two pieces of sash,

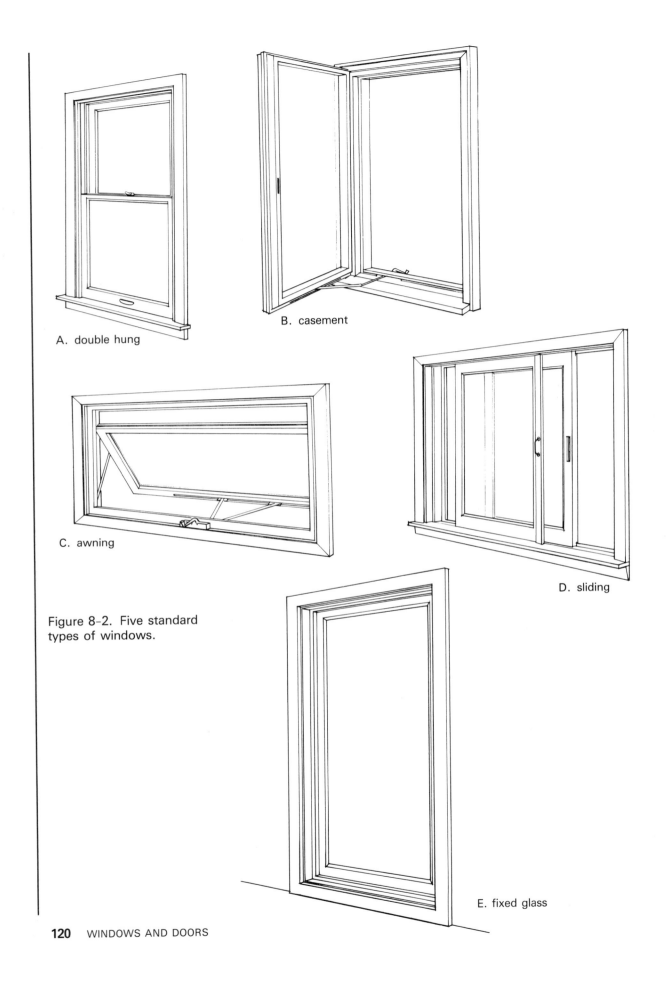

A. double hung

B. casement

C. awning

D. sliding

Figure 8-2. Five standard types of windows.

E. fixed glass

one fixed and the other sliding to the side. They are similar to double hungs in their airtightness.

Individual pieces of sash are also available for building fixed or custom windows. The sash is simply placed in a site-built jamb and sill frame. Fixed windows are not only inexpensive, but they also have negligible air infiltration since they can be completely sealed.

Buying Windows

Most factory-built windows today come with insulating or *thermapane* glass. Triple and quadruple glazing as well as special energy-saving coatings also are available, but usually for a steep price. Windows can be purchased in wood or wood with a vinyl clad exterior for lower maintenance. Metal windows that are low-cost and energy-efficient are also available. Make sure, however, that they are *thermally broken*, which means there is an insulating barrier between the outside and inside metal frame. Otherwise, metal windows will ice up and sweat, damaging interior trim and walls.

The usual source for buying windows is your building supplier. When you order a window you must specify the type of glass, the width of the jambs, and whether you want exterior casings, screens, or dividing grills. Double pane insulating glass is standard; jamb width is either 4½ inches for 2 × 4 walls or 6½ inches for 2 × 6 walls.

Another source for windows is a contractor who may either have old recycled units that have been salvaged from a house, or new units that were ordered for a job but not used. Recycled windows that are not too old can be reglazed and painted to look almost brand new. If the sills and jambs are rotten, the sash can be removed and used for fixed windows. New windows that are sitting in a builder's inventory are the best find of all since they are often sold at 25 percent or more off the builder's wholesale price.

Window Installation

Windows are installed after the building has been framed and the sheathing put on the walls. The exterior casings on the window are normally nailed directly on top of the sheathing and then the finish siding is butted against the casings. However, with vertical board siding that has no sheathing under it, the windows go on directly over the siding.

Factory-made windows with exterior casings are easily installed following the manufacturer's directions. Run a bead of caulk around the window opening before installing the window. This bead will adhere to the back of the casings and form an airtight seal. Then the window is simply inserted in the rough opening, checked for level and square, and secured with galvanized casement nails through the exterior casing.

If you have ordered windows without exterior casings, they

must be secured in a different manner until the casings can be put on. The window is inserted in the rough opening and the outside of the jamb set flush with the building's sheathing. Shim shingles are then inserted between the side jamb and the window stud to wedge the window in place so it is level and square. Finish nails are then driven through the side jambs and shims into the window stud. In double hung windows, make sure you do not nail through the track in which the sash slides.

check jambs for square

shim between jamb and stud

check sill for level

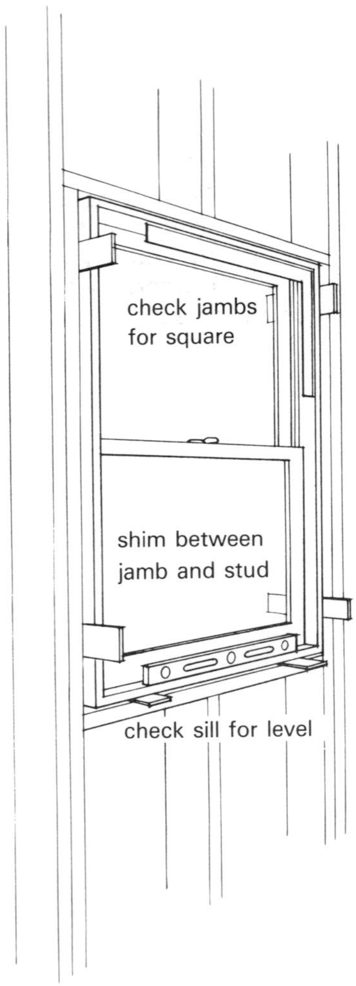

Figure 8-3. Installing a pre-hung window.

Installing Pre-hung Windows

Installing windows is a job for two people. One should be outside to hold the window in place, and the other inside shimming it until it is level and square. To install a window you will need a hammer, drill, 2-foot level, rafter square, shim shingles, caulk and caulk gun, and some 10d galvanized casement nails.

On the outside of the building, apply a thick bead of caulk around the window opening where the casing will sit. Then set the window in the rough opening. If the window is above the ground floor, it can be carried up inside the building rather than on a ladder, passed through the opening at an angle, and then pulled back in place.

Check that the sill is level while a helper keeps a firm hand on the window to keep it from falling out. Use shim shingles under the sill to get the window exactly level. Next check the top corners of the jambs for squareness using the rafter square set inside the jambs. Use shims again to wedge between the rough opening and the side jamb to get the window square.

When the jambs read square, pre-drill a nail hole through the top corner of the casing. Drive a nail just enough to secure the window while still leaving enough showing so it can be pulled out if necessary. Check that the sill is level and the jambs are square again. If the window is still good, pre-drill and drive nails in the other three corners of the casings.

Now check the operation of the window to make sure it opens smoothly and that the sash sits evenly on the weatherseals. If the sash doesn't open easily or sit well, check to see what is out of level or square, pull your nails, and start over again. Normally, factory-made windows have special restraints across the jambs to keep them square until they are installed so that sash binding is not a problem.

When you are sure the window is positioned correctly and operates well, you can nail the casings every 8 inches on center (o.c.), sink your nails, and then fill the holes with a dab of caulk. Most windows come with an aluminum drip cap that goes over the top casing to shed water and keep it from getting behind the casing. This is normally an L-shaped piece that sits on top of the casing and under the siding that butts against the window. It is always a good idea to run a bead of caulk along the back of the top casing even when it is covered with a drip cap.

Jamb extensions. In pole buildings, where the walls are built around the poles, the walls will often be considerably thicker than 6½ inches which is the largest wall width for jambs on pre-hung windows. This can be remedied by adding extension jambs to the existing window jambs to bring them out flush to the inner wall surface. Extension jambs are site-made from 1× clear pine, ripped on a table saw to the proper width. They are then glued to the jambs of the window unit and nailed to the side of the window opening.

Fixed glass installation. Installing fixed glass windows requires that you make site-built jambs, sill, and casing. This is easily done using clear 1× pine and a table saw. Let's take a look at how 32×76 patio replacement units would be installed, such as those used on our pole cabin, detailed in Part 2 of this book.

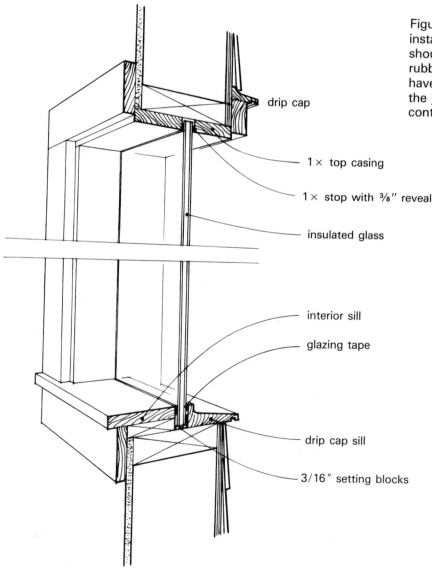

drip cap

1× top casing

1× stop with ⅜″ reveal

insulated glass

interior sill

glazing tape

drip cap sill

3/16″ setting blocks

Figure 8-4. Fixed glass installation detail. Fixed glass should always rest on two rubber setting blocks and have ¼ inch clearance from the jambs for expansion and contraction.

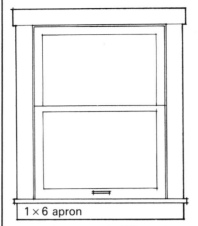

1 × 6 top casing
with ¾″ extension

1 × 6 apron

1 × 6 stool with ¾″ overhang

1 × 4 ranch casing

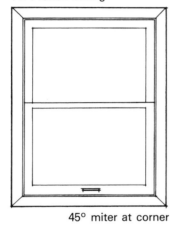

45° miter at corner

Figure 8-5. Two styles of interior window trim.

First, the interior jambs are installed. These are made from 1 × 4 pine (3½ inches wide) and they are nailed to the inside of the rough opening to form a square box that the window rests against. The inside edge of the jamb overhangs the wall framing by ½-inch because we are going to put ½-inch drywall on the inside. We want the jambs to line up with the finished wall, so we can nail the casings to the jambs. We use shim shingles as necessary behind the jambs to make sure they are plumb and square.

With the interior jambs in place, we can set the piece of fixed glass in the opening against the jambs. Two setting blocks of hard rubber are used under the window to equally carry the weight. Setting blocks must be used to prevent damage to the bottom seal of thermapane windows. When the window is sitting on the blocks there is an even gap of about ¼-inch all around the window for expansion and contraction of the glass.

Butyl glazing tape is then applied to the outside face of the window to form an airtight seal and to compensate for expansion and contraction of the window against the jambs. When the tape is in place, attach two temporary blocks on either side of the window to hold it in place.

The exterior jambs can now be ripped on the table saw to the proper width. Measure from the glazing tape to the outside of the sheathing and add ⅛-inch. This will give you the width of the jambs when they are pressed in place against the glazing tape with a little extra to make sure they extend out to the sheathing. Install the top and bottom jambs first, remove the temporary holding blocks on the side, and then install the side jambs.

The window is now secure, but we should add one more trim piece on the bottom to make sure water does not build up on the bottom sill. To do this, cut a piece of factory milled wooden drip cap to fit between the side jambs, attach a piece of glazing tape to its back, and then nail the drip cap in place against the window. Silicone caulk is used to seal its edge seams and the top joint with the window glass, so water cannot get behind the bottom drip cap.

Site-built windows. Site-built operable windows can be made in much the same way. For operable windows, the jambs form a box that extends from the inside wall surface to the exterior sheathing. A piece of sash is then hinged or set in tracks inside the jambs.

A hinged-sash window is one of the easiest types of home-made windows to build. As in figure 8–6, a sash box is made with two side jambs and a top jamb of 1× pine and a bottom sill made from 2× stock. The sill is beveled with a hand plane on the outside to shed water. The jamb box is first nailed together and then placed in the rough opening. It should be shimmed against the studs just like a normal window unit to get the jambs plumb and square.

A piece of sash can then be mounted inside the box with side hinges attached to the jamb. Wooden weatherstrip molding is then nailed to the jambs and sill to form a stop that the window closes

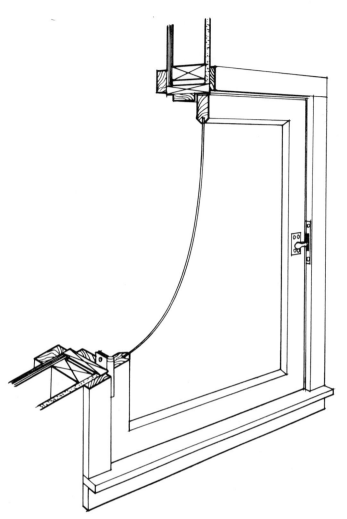

Figure 8-6. Details for a site-built hinged window.

against. Add a spring latch on the inside, and you have an inexpensive, weather-tight window.

For site-built windows, you must make and install the exterior casings yourself. Casings are usually made from 1 × 4 or 1 × 6 pine and are nailed over the jambs to cover the gap between the jambs and the window studs. It is common to leave a ⅜-inch *reveal* on the jambs, which means the casings leave ⅜-inch on the inside of the jamb exposed. The side casings are beveled on the bottom to sit tightly on the sloped sill, and the top casing sits directly on top of the side casings.

Because factory-made windows often come with narrow *brickmold* casings which don't match the architectural style of a building, you may want to order them without exterior casings and make your own. Make sure you order a *long horn* sill that has 5½-inch extensions on the side to accomodate casing widths up to 5½ inches. The ear extensions can be cut back to match whatever width of casing you are using. You can, of course, order different casings from the factory, but you'll often wind up paying an extra $4 to $5 per foot of casing for a special order.

Doors

Exterior Doors

There are three basic types of exterior doors: hinged, sliding, and overhead. Each has specific uses and advantages.

Hinged doors are commonly used in residential and commercial buildings for pedestrian entrances. They are available in wood, metal, or glass. Solid wooden doors are usually uninsulated, whereas metal doors can have a foam core that gives an R-value of up to 10. Many different glass patterns are available, with double insulated glass now being standard. Factory-made doors come pre-hung with jambs, sills, exterior casings, and weatherstripping, much like window units.

The standard size for a building entrance is 3 feet wide and 6 feet 8 inches tall. There are narrower sizes, but the standard size allows large appliances such as washers, dryers, and refrigerators to be moved through them. When ordering a pre-hung door, you must specify the jamb width and handing in addition to the width and height. Standard jamb widths are 4½ inches for 2 × 4 walls and 6½ inches for 2 × 6 walls. As with window units, this allows coverage of ½-inch sheathing and ½-inch drywall. *Handing* refers to how a door swings, either left or right. Figure 8–8 shows how to determine the handing of doors.

Because modern factory-made metal doors are so durable and energy-efficient, they are the usual choice for building entrances. It is possible to make your own insulated wooden door, however, if you have a limited budget and some time. The sidebar on page 128 shows how to make a plywood door with a foam core that would be suitable for a cabin or barn. The same method can be used with better materials, such as tongue-and-groove maple or cherry, to produce an architectural grade door that would complement any house.

Glass patio *sliding doors* are used where natural lighting, solar heat gain, or a particular view is important. Because they are glass and because their weather seals cannot be as tight since they slide, they are much less energy-efficient than a normal door, even an uninsulated wood one. Often today, hinged double glass terrace doors are used instead of sliders because they have less air infiltration.

Another type of sliding door is one that rolls on an overhead track such as the traditional barn door. This and the *overhead door* are the only practical types of wide doors. Because of the weight of a hinged door on its side hinges, hinged doors over 4 feet wide must have enormously large and strong hinges. It is easier to support a door along its entire length and let it slide from side to side or up and down. Thus sliding and overhead doors are widely used on barns and warehouses where trucks and other large equipment must enter.

A beautifully detailed double door entrance.

A glass terrace door with only one operable side is an energy-efficient way to let sunlight in and open up good views.

A sliding barn door made from rough 1 × 6 boards.

2 × 4 frame

1½″ polystyrene foam

¼″ A/C plywood skin

Building an Insulated Door

You can build your own insulated door using a 2 × 4 frame, ¼-inch A/C plywood, and 1½-inch polystyrene foam insulation (blueboard). The total cost of materials and hardware should be about $60 and will give you a door with an R-9 insulation value. The instructions below are for a 3′ × 6′ 8″ door.

First, make the 2 × 4 frame. This consists of two side pieces 80 inches long and three cross pieces that are 29 inches long. The middle cross piece should be set 40 inches from the bottom. Use 3-inch drywall screws that are countersunk into the side pieces by 1½ inches to assemble the frame. Using screws helps pull the piece tightly together and keep them from working apart.

Next, cut two pieces of 1½-inch polystyrene foam that measure 29 × 34¾ inches. These pieces should fit snugly into the 2 × 4 frame.

Cut two pieces of ¼-inch A/C plywood to cover the entire 36 × 80-inch frame. Apply a structural foam adhesive with a caulking gun to the back C side of each piece of plywood. Position the plywood pieces over the 2 × 4 frame and foam so they line up exactly with the frame.

Use scrap pieces of 2 × 4 placed on both sides of the door and clamps to squeeze the two pieces of plywood to the frame. You will need about twelve pieces of 3-foot 2 × 4s and twelve clamps to make six clamping bars that will give a good seal between the plywood and the frame. Let the adhesive set up for a day in a warm spot before removing the clamping bars.

The door can then be sanded and finished with paint or stain, the frame drilled out for a lockset, and the hinges mortised into the frame.

Wooden sliding doors are very easy to make on site, using either plywood or 1× boards put on a Z-frame. Sliding doors are usually mounted on the outside of a building so they will not hit obstructions as they slide along the wall. Often wide sliding doors are built in two pieces, so either half may be opened with less effort.

Overhead garage-type doors are used in similar situations for vehicle entrances. They are mounted on side tracks with rollers, and slide conveniently away overhead. These doors are made from a series of hinged panels and because of the complexity of their operation, they are less suited to being site-built.

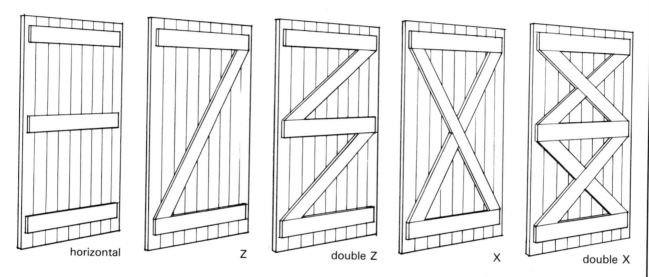

horizontal   Z   double Z   X   double X

Interior Doors

There are four basic types of interior wooden doors that are available as solid wood or hollow-core units. *Hollow-core* doors are made of veneer plywood glued over a honey comb interior frame. They are light and inexpensive, but also more fragile than solid wood doors. Interior doors are also available as completely set up units with *split* jambs and casings for both sides of the door, or as individual doors that can be hung on site-built jambs with custom casing.

Hinged doors are available in widths from 24 to 36 inches and standard heights of 6′ 6″ and 6′ 8″. The standard size for residential construction is 2′ 8″ × 6′ 8″. For wide openings, french doors can be used, which consist of two sets of doors which swing in opposite directions.

Bi-fold doors are hinged doors with folding sections that fold neatly out of the way when open. These come in louvered or paneled styles and are used for closet doors, laundry rooms, and other enclosures that need wide access and ventilation.

There are two types of *sliding* doors available; one slides on the outside of a wall and the other, a *pocket* door, slides into a cavity in the wall. Pocket doors are extremely useful for openings that are usually open, where a hinged door would be in the way. Of course,

Figure 8-7. Simple site-built doors can be made from vertical boards held together with back bracing.

the wall pocket which the door slides into, must be free of obstructions such as wiring, plumbing, and framing. Because of the non-loadbearing walls in pole structures, pocket doors can be used extensively to hide doors and open up more floor space.

Installing a Site-Built Door

For barn and outbuilding construction, building your own doors or hanging recycled ones is often the most economical way to go. This means you must install your own door jambs and then hang the door with hinges.

Jambs are made from pine boards that are wide enough to span the width of the wall including any siding or wall covering. For light interior doors, nominal 1-inch stock is used, for heavier exterior doors, 5/4-inch stock (a little under 1¼ inches thick) should be used. Of course, for barns and other utility buildings, 2 × 6s or 2 × 8s could be used for a heavy door jamb.

First, cut the top jamb to the width of the rough opening. Tack it in place with a couple of finish nails driven part way in. Then use shim shingles driven from both sides between it and the top of the rough opening to move it down to the proper door height. The height of the top jamb off the finished floor needs to be the door height plus ⅜-inch for clearance. Make a mark on one side of the rough opening at this height and then shim the top jamb down until it is at this mark and level. The jamb can now be permanently nailed in place. There should be three sets of shims behind the top jamb, a set at each corner and one in the middle.

Next, cut the two side jambs. These will extend from the floor to the top jamb and thus will be ⅜-inch longer than the door height. These should be set plumb with four sets of shims behind them. Make sure the finished opening between the two jambs is ¼-inch larger than the door width.

If you are building an exterior door that has a threshold, this should now be cut and nailed in place between the jambs. A 5/4-inch piece of oak makes an excellent and durable threshold. Remember to cut the door down in height to compensate for the height of the threshold.

The door can now be hung. Most exterior doors have three sets of 3½-inch hinges on them to support the weight of the door. Because site-built doors tend to be heavy (especially when compared to hollow-core units), it is advisable to use three hinges on interior doors as well.

The edge of the door should be mortised out to accept the leaf of the hinge. Set the top and bottom hinges 8 inches on center (o.c.) from the top and bottom of the door. The middle hinge goes directly in the center of the door. Mark the outline of the hinge leaf with a pencil and then mortise this out to the depth of the leaf with a ¾-inch chisel. The hinges can then be screwed into place, flush with the frame of the door.

Carefully set the door in place between the jambs and use shim shingles underneath the door to raise it up ¼-inch off the floor or threshold. Adjust the shims so there is an even ⅛-inch gap between the top of the door and the top jamb. With a pencil, mark the position of the hinges on the side jamb and then remove the door from the opening.

The jambs can now be mortised for the hinges using the marks on the jamb to determine their proper height. Take the pins out of the hinges and take them apart so you can hold the leafs in place against the side jamb to mark them. Mortise and screw the leafs into the jamb. The door can now be put in place and the hinges should fit together. Drop the hinge pins back in and the door is mounted.

There should be an even ⅛-inch gap on the sides and top of the door. If not, the jambs must be bent or the hinges not properly mortised into place. Both the jambs and the hinges can be re-shimmed if necessary.

When the door fits well, cut a piece of 1× pine for the stop. The stop is the piece of wood the door closes against and is nailed onto the side and top jambs. The door can then be drilled for a lockset and a strike plate mortised into the side jamb.

Door Installation

Installing pre-hung door units is very similar to installing factory window units. The unit is set in the rough opening, is shimmed until it is plumb and square, and then nailed in place through the jambs with casing or finish nails. Exterior doors are set in place after the sheathing, but before the siding, just like windows. Interior pre-hung doors are set in place after the drywall or wall covering has been finished.

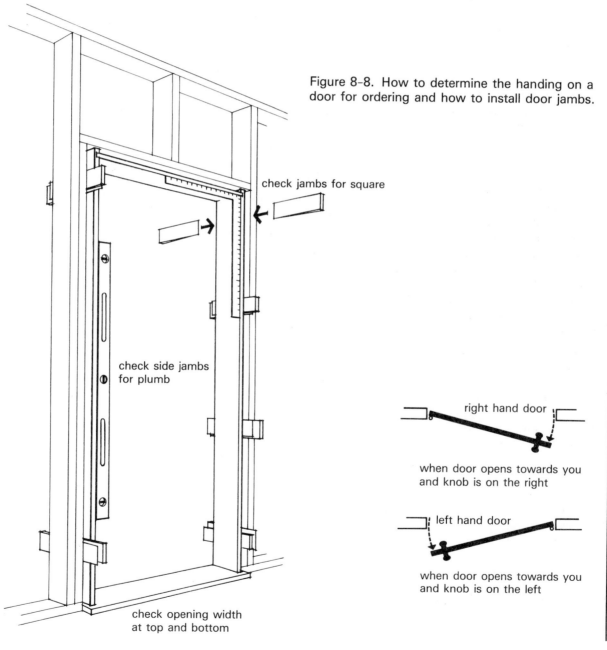

Figure 8-8. How to determine the handing on a door for ordering and how to install door jambs.

check jambs for square

check side jambs for plumb

check opening width at top and bottom

right hand door

when door opens towards you and knob is on the right

left hand door

when door opens towards you and knob is on the left

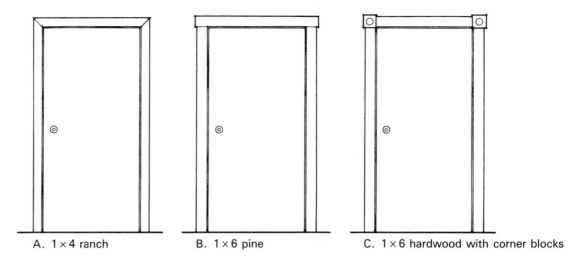

A. 1 × 4 ranch   B. 1 × 6 pine   C. 1 × 6 hardwood with corner blocks

Figure 8–9. Three styles of interior door casing.

If you are hanging your own doors to save money or because you are using recycled doors, then you must cut and install the jambs and casings yourself. For heavy exterior doors, it is advisable to use 5/4 pine or fir for the jambs which is 1¼ inches thick. This will give you a sturdier frame to hang the door on, and will not let the door sag over time with repeated use. For interior doors, which are much lighter, ¾-inch jambs are suitable.

You can chose from many casing styles including the standard ranch molding that is on pre-hung doors or 1 × 6 pine boards, or fancier molded casings. The casings can also be joined in several ways. Figure 8–9 shows three standard details with different kinds of casings.

Part II/Building Plans

Lean-To Animal Shelter

This is a simple, inexpensive lean-to barn that can serve as an animal shelter, a barn for hay storage, or as a carport. It can be built by two people in several days.

The pole foundation consists of 6 × 6 pressure-treated posts that are available at any building supply outlet. They are set at a depth of 5 feet in the ground with a 12-inch concrete necklace.

The siding is rough-sawn board and batten spruce, but ½-inch plywood siding could also be used. The open front side of the building is oriented to the south to catch the sun and to shelter the animals from the northern winter wind.

The roof is a conventional shed design with a large overhang in front to keep rain out of the building. The slope is designed to use exactly 16-foot 2 × 10 rafters, since this is the longest standard lumber that is available.

This building could easily be turned into a horse or cow barn by adding a front wall, doors, and windows. This design has a floating concrete slab in one of the bays which serves as a dry platform for feeding the animals or storing equipment.

To use this building as a carport, it needs to be at least 16 feet deep. This would mean adding one extra pole on each side, to break the side spans into two 8-foot sections. The rafters would also have to be broken into two sections that rest on a center rafter girt.

LEAN-TO ANIMAL SHELTER SPECIFICATIONS

Dimensions:	30′ × 12′, 360 sq.ft.
Poles:	(8) 6 × 6 p.t. posts
Framing:	Sill girt, 2 × 10 p.t. Siding girts, 2 × 6 24″ o.c. w/2 × 4 brace Rafter girts, (2) 2 × 10 Rafters, 2 × 10 24″ o.c., 16′ length
Roofing:	1 × 3 strapping 24″ o.c. Galvanized metal roofing
Siding:	Rough 1 × 8 spruce board and batten
Floors:	10′ × 11′ floating concrete slab in first bay; packed clay in others

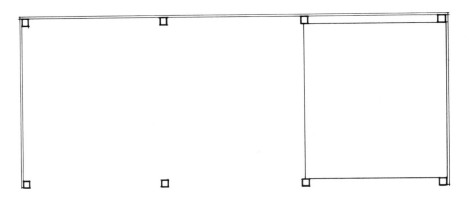

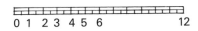

0 1 2 3 4 5 6   12

Pole and floor plan

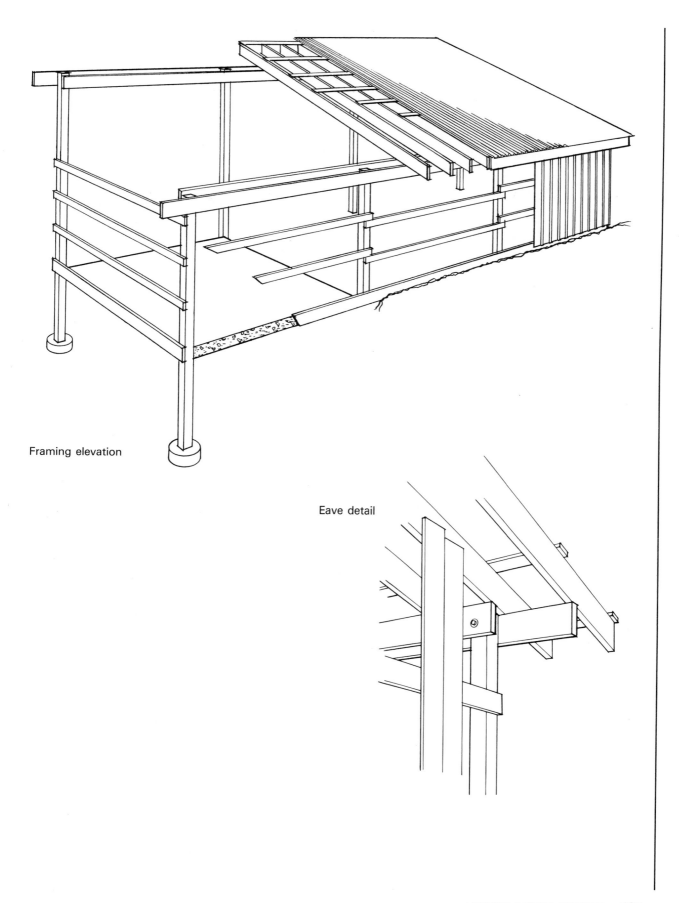

Framing elevation

Eave detail

Two Horse Stable

This is a 20 × 24 horse stable that provides two stables and a feeding/tack storage area. It is built with 6 × 6 pressure-treated posts for easy assembly and with economical green, rough-sawn lumber.

The floor is green 2 × 8 spruce laid on a bed of crushed stone. This provides good footing for the horses, good drainage, and is durable. A concrete floor is not recommended because it can be slippery when wet and would have to have expensive floor drains.

The interior is also sided with green 2 × 8 to protect the framing and divide the two stables. In most climates insulation will be unnecessary because of the large amount of heat given off by the horses. Six inches of fiberglass could be put in the walls and ceiling in extreme cold climates. Care should be taken to install a vapor barrier over all the insulation and to provide for adequate ventilation, if the ceiling is closed off to hold insulation.

The windows are inexpensive awning units that are covered with a heavy wire mesh on the inside to protect the glass. The doors are site-built units made from 1 × 6 shiplap siding with a double X brace on their back.

The roof is a simple 5:12 gable with a conventional ridge board rather than a ridge girt. To help stiffen the roof, 2 × 6 collar ties are put on every other pair of rafters. These serve as ceiling framing if the attic space is closed off. These collar ties overlap and rest on a center girt that runs the length of the building.

Again, this building could easily serve as a garage or workshed. The only modification might be to pour a concrete slab and eliminate the center dividing wall.

TWO HORSE STABLE SPECIFICATIONS

Dimensions:	20' × 24', 480 sq.ft.
Poles:	(18) 6 × 6 p.t. posts, 14' long
Framing:	Sill girt, 2 × 10 p.t. Siding girts, 2 × 6 24" o.c. Rafter girts, (2) 2 × 10 Collar tie girts, (2) 2 × 6 Rafters, 2 × 8 24" o.c. w/2 × 10 ridge plate Collar ties, 2 × 6 48" o.c. w/ply. gusset
Roofing:	½" CDX plywood deck 15 lb. roofing felt, 5" galv. drip edge 235 lb. fiberglass shingles
Siding:	1 × 6 vertical shiplap spruce 2 × 8 rough spruce interior wall covering
Trim:	1 × 8 spruce fascia (2) 1 × 6 spruce soffit boards 1 × 4 spruce corner boards and casings
Floors:	2 × 8 rough spruce on crushed stone bed
Insulation:	None
Doors:	(2) double Z-frame spruce doors (6—0 × 6—8) (1) 3–0 × 6–8 wood w/top lites
Windows:	(3) 32 × 20 awning windows w/metal grill on inside

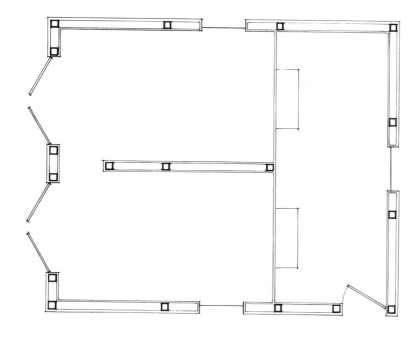

Pole and floor plan

0 1 2 3 4 5 6   12

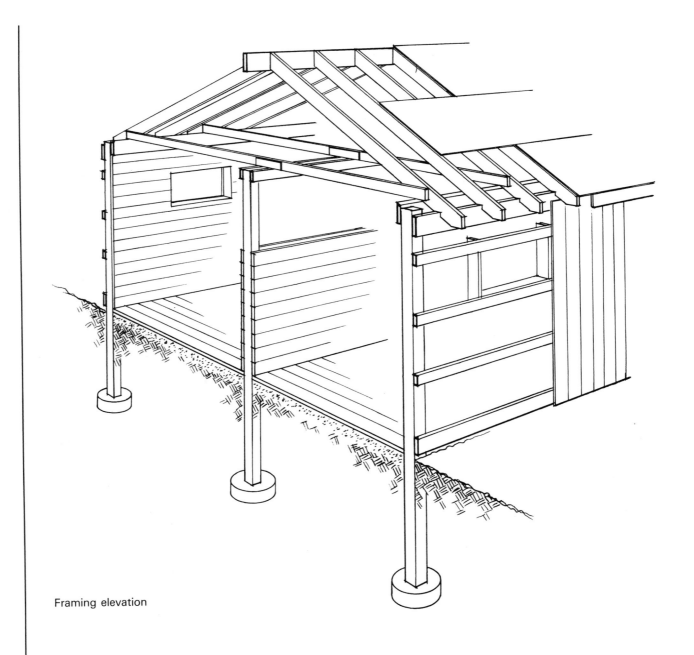

Framing elevation

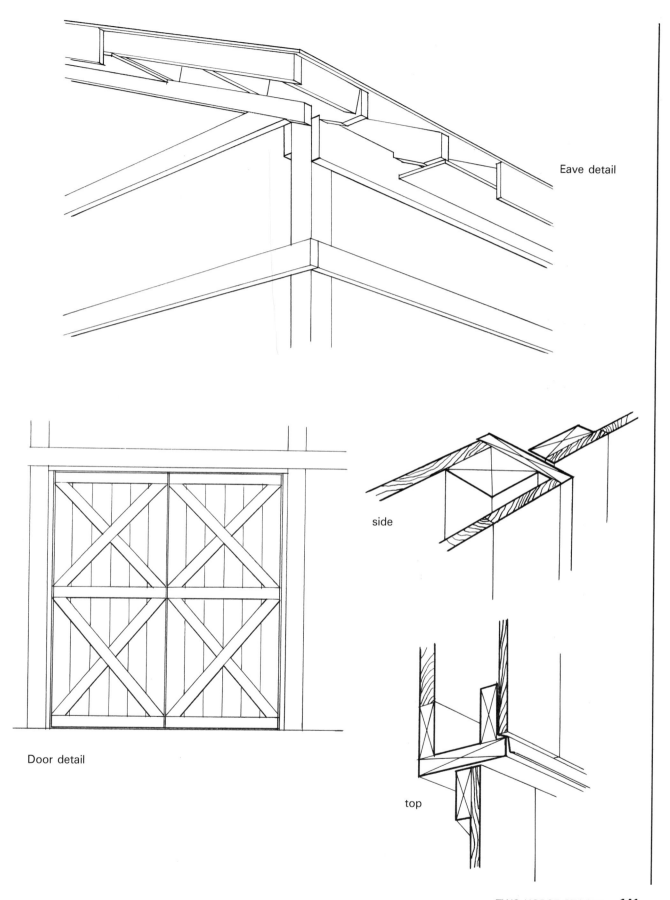

Eave detail

Door detail

side

top

Two Car Garage/Woodshed

This building serves the dual functions of providing a place to store your cars and your yearly supply of wood. It does this with a large roof overhang on the sides of the building that can accomodate over four cords of wood apiece. In addition, there is an 18×22 attic space that can be used to store the overflow from the house attic or as a studio.

This building again uses 6×6 pressure-treated posts for the frame since they do not need to be over 16 feet in length and their four planed sides make finish work much easier. A 21×17 concrete slab is poured inside of the posts with a slight pitch to drain towards the doors.

To eliminate any interior posts and to carry the second floor joists, a 10-inch steel I-beam is used. A wooden girt system could be used, but it would need a center post for support which might interfere with opening car doors. Since a steel I-beam only adds about $50 to the cost of materials over the cost of using a girt system, it seems well justified.

Use 2×10 floor joists spaced 24 inches on center (o.c.) to line up with the roof rafters. This is necessary because the rafter run is over 16 feet in length and the main rafters must have a cripple rafter nailed on them to form the roof overhang. By lining up the joists with the rafters, the cantilevered joist extensions can serve as the bottom nailer for the cripple rafters. The joists are joined with a plywood gusset where they meet on top of the steel I-beam.

There is a fold-away stair unit that provides access to the second floor. This means the left-hand car bay must be empty to pull down the stairs, but it is an economical solution in terms of space and money. As an alternative, an outside stairway could be built on the rear of the building with a door replacing the double-hung window. This would make sense if the attic area were being used regularly as a studio.

Standard 8 × 7 overhead garage doors are used on the front. The rear windows are 4-foot wide sliding units that are mounted 4 feet off the ground so a workbench or tool storage area can be put under them. There are no windows on the sides, of course, since there will be wood piled against the sides of the building. Double-hung windows are used in the attic area for light and ventilation.

GARAGE/WOODSHED SPECIFICATIONS

Dimensions:	Overall, 30′ × 20′ w/roof overhangs Garage, 22′ × 18′ w/2nd floor storage Roof, 19′ × 20′ gable, 760 sq.ft.
Poles:	(8) 6 × 6 p.t. posts, 16′ length (6) 6 × 6 p.t. posts, 14′ length
Framing:	Sill girt, 2 × 10 p.t. Siding girts, 2 × 4 24″ o.c. Floor girts, (2) 2 × 8 on outside walls W10 × 19 lb. steel I-beam in center Rafter girts, (2) 2 × 8 Floor joists, 2 × 10 24″ o.c. w/plywood gusset Studs, 2 × 4 on gable end Rafters, 2 × 10 24″ o.c. w/cripples for overhang
Roofing:	½″ CDX plywood decking 15 lb. roofing felt, 5″ galv. drip edge 235 lb. fiberglass shingles
Siding:	1 × 6 vertical shiplap spruce
Trim:	1 × 8 spruce fascia w/crown molding ½″ A/C plywood soffit 1 × 4 spruce corner boards and casings
Floors:	21′ × 17′ 4″ floating concrete slab ¾″ plywood underlayment on 2nd floor
Insulation:	None
Doors:	(2) 7–0 × 8–0 overhead garage doors (1) fold-away stair unit to attic
Windows:	(2) 48 × 36 sliding units in garage (2) 24 × 46 double hung units in attic

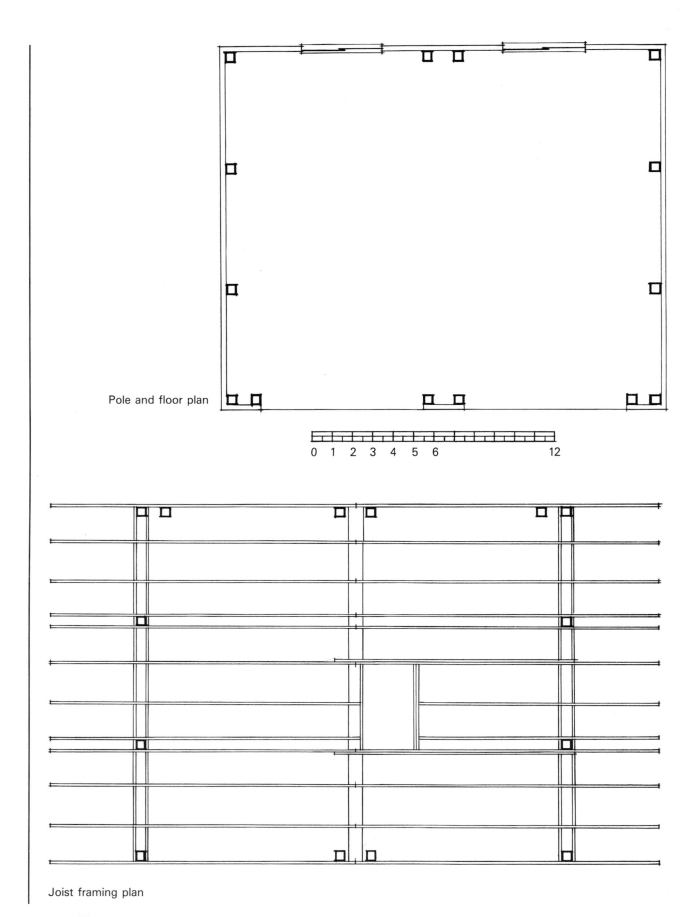

Pole and floor plan

0 1 2 3 4 5 6 12

Joist framing plan

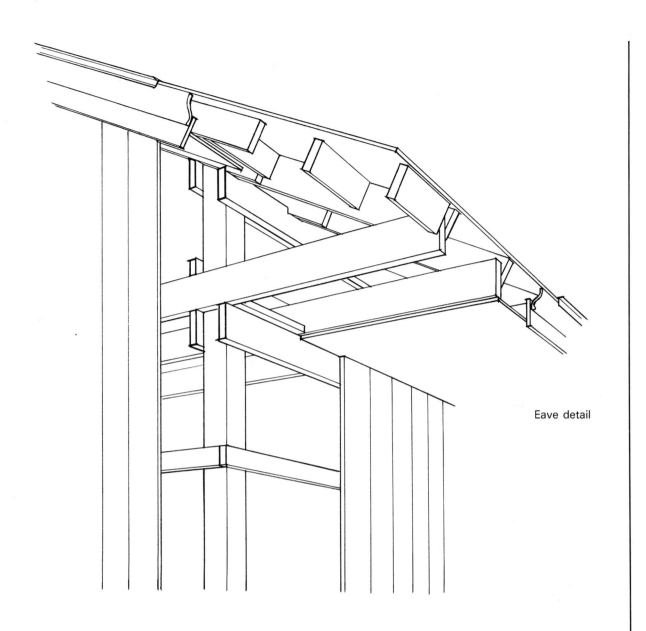

Eave detail

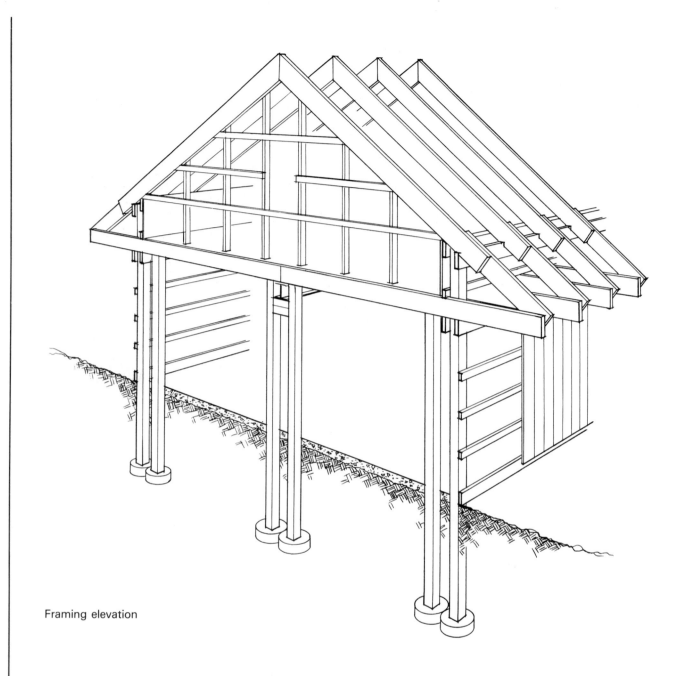

Framing elevation

Pole Cabin

This design is a small 18×18 cabin with a larger 24×24 hip roof that covers a wrap-around porch. There is one large living space that combines kitchen, living, and eating areas. A loft over the kitchen provides a sleeping area for sleeping bags on mattresses.

The cabin is designed with well-insulated walls and passive solar heating for a cold climate. The south wall is completely glazed with patio door replacement units which are inexpensive, tempered glass units. A skylight in the south roof lets in light to the loft area and provides summer ventilation.

The cabin's north and east walls are built around the 6-inch poles and insulated with two 3½-inch batts of fiberglass, one run horizontally behind the studs and the other vertically in the stud bays. The south and west walls are free-standing walls that are framed with 2×6s that extend up to the roof rafters.

The first floor is framed with 2×8 joists that sit on 2×12 floor girts. The joists for the south half of the floor and the porch area on the western side should be pressure-treated, since they extend out from under the enclosed cabin area. The floor girts that are exposed under the porches should also be pressure-treated.

The finish flooring is 2×6 tongue-and-groove fir which is installed directly over the floor joists. The fir flooring ends under the south and west walls of the cabin, and pressure-treated 2×6s, spaced $\frac{1}{8}$-inch for drainage, continue out as decking on the porch. The interior walls and cathedral ceiling are finished with 1×6 shiplap pine that has been planed on one side. Both the siding and roofing are cedar shingles that blend in with the surrounding environment and require no maintenance.

POLE CABIN SPECIFICATIONS

Dimensions:	Overall, 24' × 24' Cabin, 18' × 18', 324 sq. ft. Loft, 18' × 9', 162 sq. ft. Roof, 26' × 26' hip, 728 sq. ft.
Poles:	(9) 20' class 6 (6" tip diameter)

Framing:	Floor girts, (2) 2 × 12 on N. and S. poles
	   dbl. 2 × 12 on center poles
	Rafter girts, dbl 2 × 12 w/extra 2 × 12 on N. wall
	Loft girts, (2) 2 × 8
	Floor joists, 2 × 8 16" o.c., p.t. where exposed
	   on deck
	Loft joists, 2 × 6 16" o.c.
	Rafters, 2 × 12 24" o.c.

Roofing:	½" CDX plywood decking 15 lb. roofing felt, 5" galv. drip edge #2 cedar shingles
Siding:	½" CDX plywood sheathing Tyvek wrap #2 cedar shingles
Trim:	1 × 8 cedar fascia and soffit w/2" vent strip 1 × 4 cedar corner boards and window casings
Floors:	2 × 6 tongue-and-groove fir planking 2 × 6 p.t. on deck
Wall Finish:	1 × 6 vertical shiplap pine
Insulation:	6" fiberglass batts in 2 × 6 walls (2) 4" fiberglass batts in N. and E. walls 6" fiberglass in floor 10" fiberglass in rafters w/foam vent shutes 1" isocyanurate foam over rafters
Doors:	(1) 3–0 × 6–8 custom wood insulated door (1) 2–8 × 6–8 insulated glass door (1) 4–0 × 6–8 wood bi-fold closet door
Windows:	(4) 32 × 76 insul. patio replacement units (1) 24 × 42 double hung (2–6 × 4–6 r.o.) (1) 32 × 20 awning (3–0 × 2–0 r.o.) (1) 22 × 38 skylight

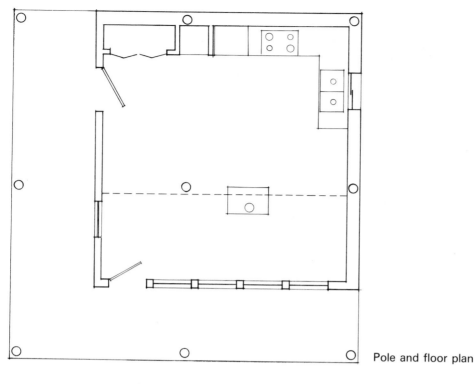

Pole and floor plan

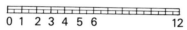
0 1 2 3 4 5 6   12

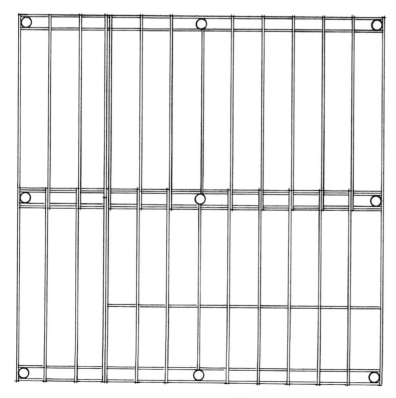

Joist framing plan

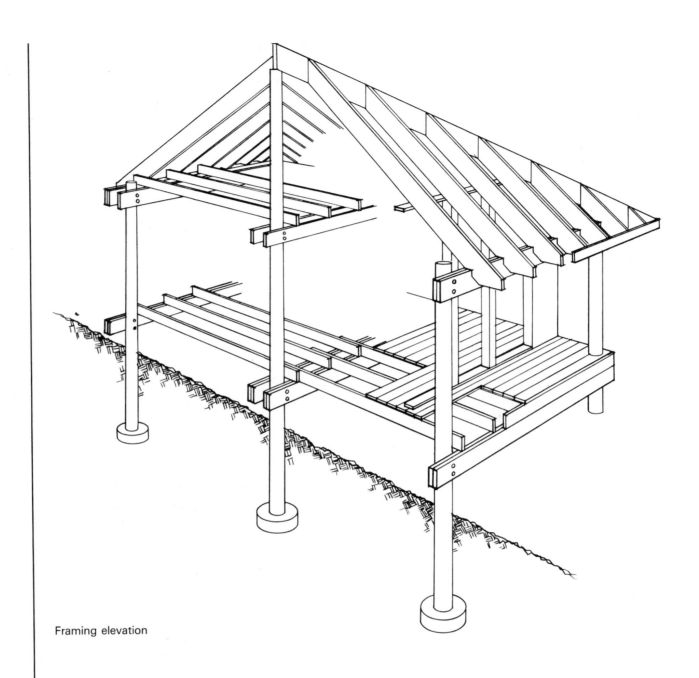

Framing elevation

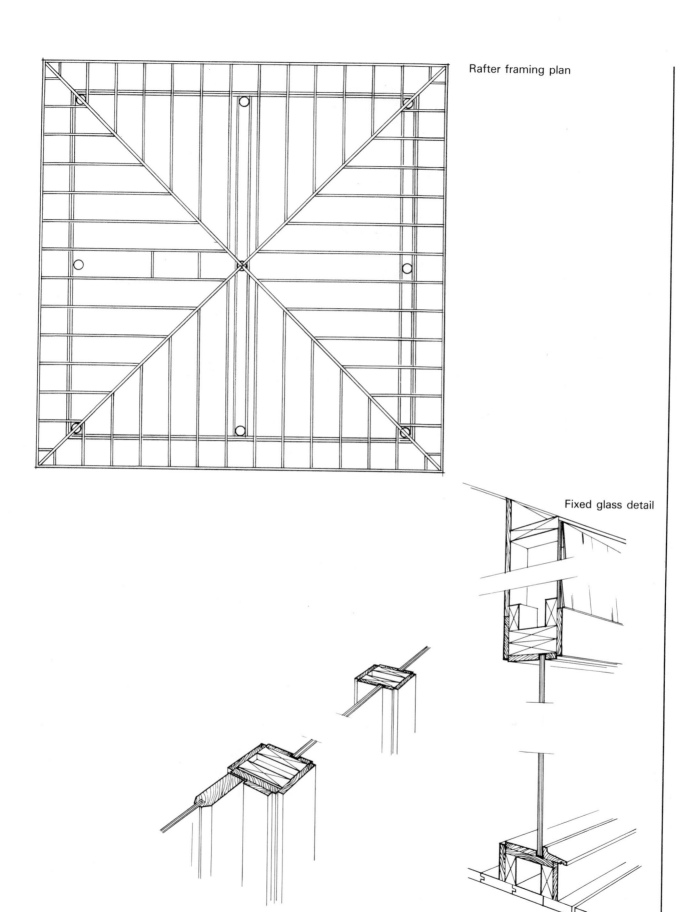

Rafter framing plan

Fixed glass detail

Hillside House

This is a two-story, two bedroom, compact house that has just slightly more than 1000 square feet of living space. It is designed to be built on a sloping hillside to accomodate a carport underneath the house. The windows and doors are mostly on the southern side of the house to take advantage of passive solar heating.

The house is framed off of nine 8-inch poles with three 6-inch poles to carry the front of the deck. All the poles are outside of the building envelope, except for the middle row of 8-inch poles. These get coated with polyurethane sealer and then boxed with pine trim.

The walls of the house are standard 2 × 6 stud walls that are framed from the plywood subflooring to the floor girts above. Blocking is put between these girts to catch the top of the wall. The wall and the girts are then covered with drywall, forming a box-like soffit detail that runs along the east and west walls.

The roof is a standard gable roof that has a 4-foot overhang in front to shelter the second floor balcony and the house entrance below. The attic ceiling joists are tied together with plywood gussets over the center girt to act as collar ties. Two layers of 6-inch fiberglass batts, laid perpendicular to one another, are used to insulate the attic. The second layer completely covers the attic joists, thus eliminating the heat loss around and through the joists that occurs when only a single thick layer of insulation is used.

The kitchen and baths are located close together in the rear of the house. This minimizes plumbing runs and the height of the insulated plumbing chase that runs from under the bath to below the frost line. A wood stove in the living room, with a metal-asbestos chimney that runs up through the attic, heats the entire house.

HILLSIDE HOUSE SPECIFICATIONS

Dimensions:	Overall, 24 ft. by 36 ft., 1050 sq. ft. First Floor, 24' × 24' with 12' × 24' deck Second Floor, 24' × 24' with 4' × 24' balcony Roof, 26' × 26' gable
Poles:	(9) 30' class 2 (8" tip diameter) (3) 20' class 6

Framing:	Floor girts, (2) 2 × 12 on E. and W. poles
	          (2) dbl. 2 × 12 on center poles
	Rafter and ceiling girts, (2) 2 × 12 on E. and W.
	            poles
	          (2) 2 × 10 on center poles
	Floor joists, 2 × 8 16" o.c.
	Attic joists, 2 × 6 16" o.c.
	Deck joists, 2 × 8 p.t. 16" o.c.
	Rafters, 2 × 8 16" o.c.
	Wall studs, 2 × 6 24" o.c.

Roofing:	½" CDX plywood decking 15 lb. roofing felt, 5" galv. drip edge 235 lb. fiberglass shingles
Siding:	Tyvek wrap over studs ½" T1–11 plywood siding
Trim:	1 × 6 pine corner boards and fascia ½" A/C plywood soffit w/2" continuous vent
Floors:	¾" plywood underlayment Deck, 2 × 6 p.t. decking
Wall Finish:	½" gypsum
Insulation:	6" fiberglass batts in floor and walls (2) 6" fiberglass batts in attic overlapped 6 mil vapor barrier on walls and 2nd fl. ceiling
Doors:	(2) 6–0 × 6–8 sliding glass patio units on S wall (1) 5–0 × 6–8 french door unit to balcony (4) 2–8 × 6–8 wood panel for bedrooms and baths (2) 2–0 × 6–8 wood panel for closets
Windows:	(8) 28 × 46 double hung units (2—10 × 4—10 r.o.) (2) 32 × 76 fixed patio replacement units

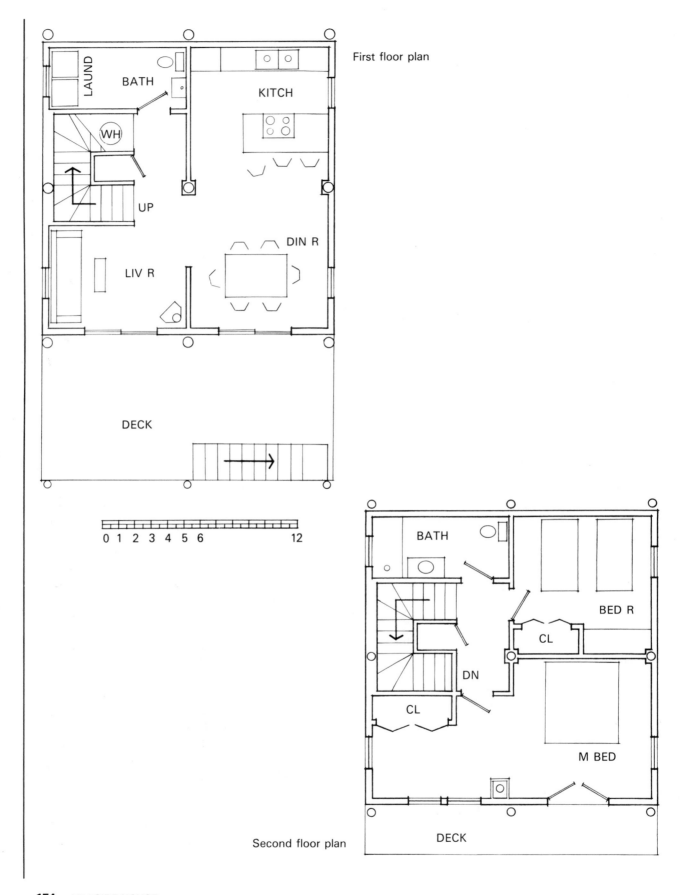

First floor plan

LAUND

BATH

KITCH

WH

UP

LIV R

DIN R

DECK

0 1 2 3 4 5 6   12

BATH

BED R

CL

DN

CL

M BED

DECK

Second floor plan

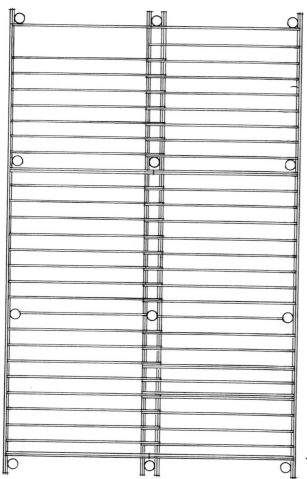

Joist framing plan

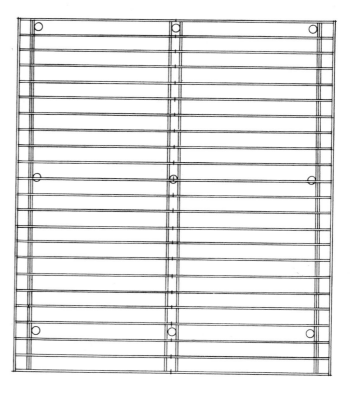

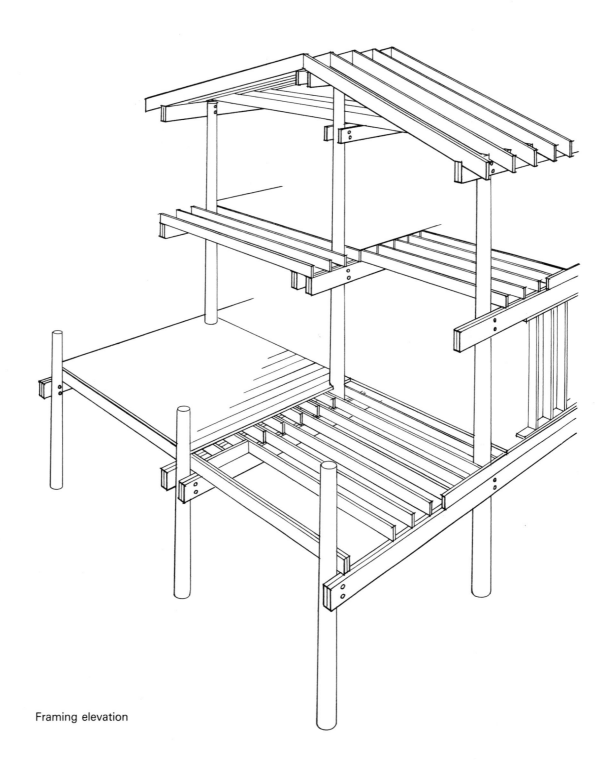

Framing elevation

Lake House

This is a warm climate house, designed to set next to a lake or estuary without disturbing the natural shore environment. It sits above the edge marsh land with a wooden walkway connecting it to a driveway, and a deck and floating dock that extend out over the water.

The house is a 16 × 32, two-story, two bedroom, saltbox design. The roof overhangs the front of the house to protect the second floor balcony and cover the two-story bay window. On the first floor, the kitchen, dining and living areas are undivided. A bath, laundry room, and utility closet are lined up against the back wall to minimize plumbing runs and take advantage of the space under the stairs. On the second floor, there are a master bedroom, guest bedroom, bath, and linen closet.

The pole frame consists of 8-inch poles, 10 feet on center (o.c.), tied together with 20-foot 4 × 14 floor girts. Given the nature of the soils along the shoreline, the poles should be set with a pole driving rig that hammers each pole into the silt and mud. The depth of embedment should be determined by an engineer after drilling test holes.

The saltbox roof is framed with a site-built truss system that sits on double 2 × 12 rafter girts. since the trusses sit every 24 inches on center (o.c.), 1 × 3 strapping is nailed on to their bottom cords, 16 inches o.c., as a nailer for the drywall ceiling. A special soffit detail, as shown in the drawings, is used to close off the soffit between the house walls and the poles before the roof trusses go on.

Sewer, water, and electrical conduits are run out of the house and along the underside of the walkway to the driveway area.

LAKE HOUSE SPECIFICATIONS

Dimensions:	Overall, 40′ × 24′ House, 32′ × 16′, 1000 sq. ft. Deck, 7′ × 24′ and 8′ × 22′ Dock, 9′ × 10′ Walkway, 4′ × 20′ Roof, 14′ × 18′, 10′ × 18′ salt box truss
Poles:	(11) class 2 (8″ tip diameter) (4) class 6 (6″ tip diameter) (4) 6 × 6 p.t. posts for walkway
Framing:	Floor girts, 4 × 14 20′ length Deck girts, (2) 2 × 12 p.t. Rafter girts, dbl. 2 × 12 Floor joists, 2 × 6 16″ o.c. w/hangers Deck joists, 2 × 6 p.t. 16″ o.c. Attic joists, 2 × 6 truss cord 24″ o.c. w/1 × 3 16″ o.c. strapping for gypsum Rafters, custom trusses 24″ o.c. Wall studs, 2 × 6 24″ o.c.
Roofing:	½″ CDX plywood decking 15 lb. roofing felt, 5″ galv. drip edge 235 lb. fiberglass shingles
Siding:	½″ CDX plywood sheathing Tyvek wrap 5½″ bevel siding, 3″ exposed to weather
Trim:	1 × 6 pine corner and fascia boards ½″ A/C plywood soffit w/2″ vent strip
Flooring:	¾″ plywood underlayment ½″ CDX under first floor joists
Wall Finish:	½″ gypsum
Insulation:	6″ fiberglass batts in floor and walls (2) 6″ fiberglass batts overlapped in attic 6 mil vapor barrier on walls and 2nd fl. ceiling

Doors:
- (1) 3–0 × 6–8 metal insulated door
- (2) 5–0 × 6–8 french doors
- (4) 2–8 × 6–8 wood panel doors for bath and bedrooms
- (1) 2–6 × 6–8 wood panel door for closet
- (2) 2–0 × 6–8 wood panel door for closet and laundry
- (1) 4–0 × 6–8 closet bi-fold
- (1) 6–0 × 6–8 closet bi-fold

Windows:
- (6) 24 × 42 double hung (2–6 × 4–6 r.o.) in bay window
- (4) 28 × 42 double hung (2–10 × 4–6 r.o.)
- (2) 20 × 32 double hung (2–2 × 3–6 r.o.) in baths
- (1) dbl. 24 × 42 (5–0 × 4–6 r.o.) in lv. room

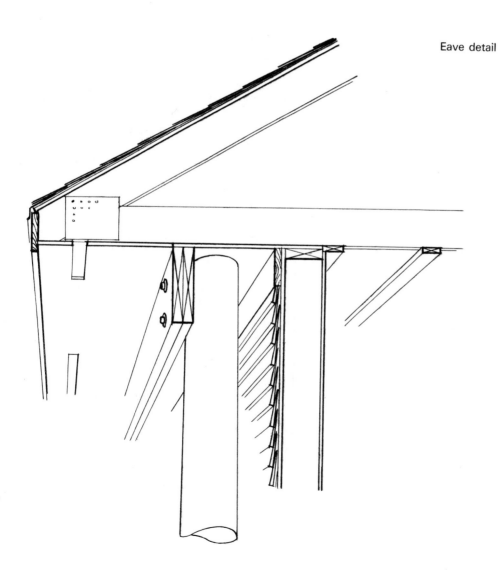

Eave detail

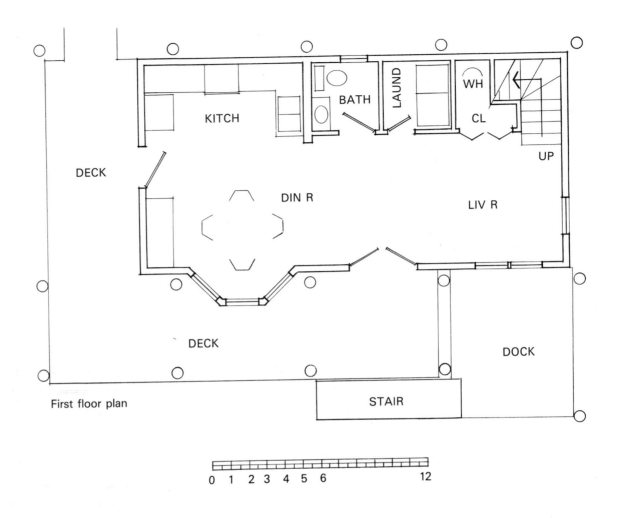

First floor plan

0 1 2 3 4 5 6   12

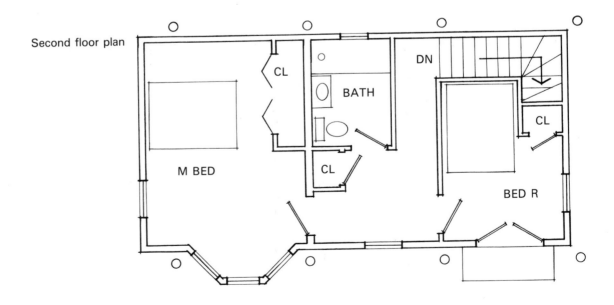

Second floor plan

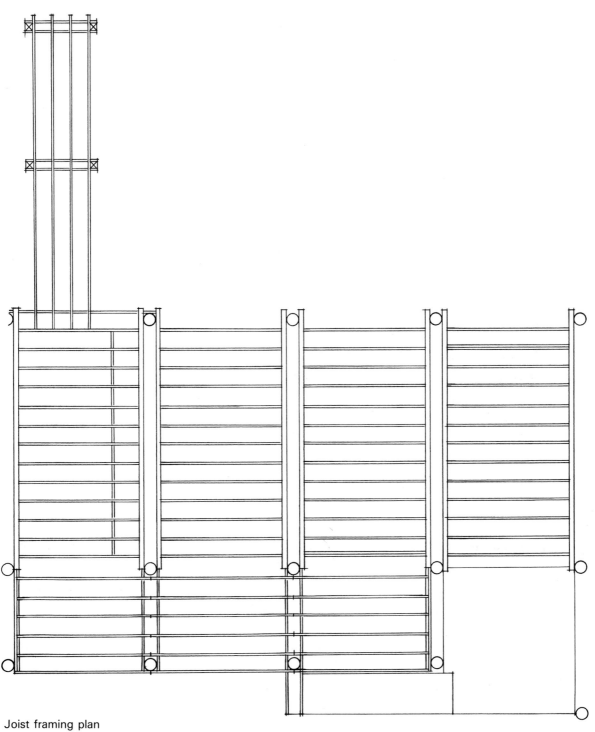

Joist framing plan

Framing elevation

APPENDIX

Further Reading

Agricultural Buildings and Structures, James Whitaker, Reston Publishing Co., 1979, Reston, Virginia 22090. This is an excellent reference book for barn builders. It presents design and construction information in a clear, straightforward manner.

Architectural Graphic Standards, Charles Ramsey and Harold Sleeper, John Wiley and Sons, Somerset, N.J., 1970. This is the bible of building details for architects. It is not a how-to book, but rather includes drawings and specifications of almost every construction detail imaginable. Check the reference section at your library for this book or similar ones. Its price tag puts it beyond the reach of all except practicing architects.

Climatic Design, Donald Watson and Kenneth Labs, McGraw-Hill Book Co., 1984, 1221 Avenue of the Americas, New York, N.Y. 10020. This is a comprehensive reference book on designing for energy-efficiency and comfort. It outlines strategies from landscaping to superinsulated walls with a wealth of climatic data and design strategies for different regions.

Engineering Soil Classification for Residential Development, FHA Bulletin No. 373, Federal Housing Administration, Washington, D.C. 20025. This is the soil classification method that is the basis of the AWPI pole embedment charts that are presented in chapter 5.

Fine Homebuilding Magazine, The Taunton Press, 52 Church Hill Rd., Newtown, Connecticut 06470. This is an excellent building magazine, showing examples of good craftsmanship and new techniques. Several pole building articles have appeared in the past several years. *Steep-Site Solution*, *Pole House in the Treetops*, and *Pressure-Treated Poles* are three articles that appeared in issue No. 15, June/July 1983. *Above The Flood* appeared in issue No. 17, October/November 1983.

FHA Pole House Construction, American Wood Preservers Institute, 2nd edition, 1980. Available from AWPI, 1945 Gallows Rd., Suite 405, Vienna, Va. 22180. Price $4.00. This is a 30-page booklet that covers the basics of pole building and the requirements for FHA financing. Ask for their free list of current publications when you write to them.

Modern Carpentry, Willis Wagner, Goodheart Wilcox Co., South Holland, Illinois. This is the standard high-school and vocational school carpentry text. It covers all phases of stud construction framing and finish work. This is a book well worth buying and keeping as a reference.

Low-Cost, Energy-Efficient Shelter, Eugene Eccli, editor, Rodale Press, Emmaus, Pennsylvania 18049. This is an excellent book to start you thinking about how to design an efficient building. It covers planning, materials, low-cost building techniques, and energy conservation. It's been around for ten years, but is still the best single source of design ideas for the owner-builder that I have seen.

Low-Cost Green Lumber Construction, Leigh Seddon, Garden Way Publishing, 1981, Storey Communciations Inc., Schoolhouse Rd., Pownal, Vermont 05261. How to save money using green, rough-cut lumber. Lots of tips on how to buy, store, and build with green wood.

Pole Building Design, Donald Patterson, 6th edition, 1981, American Wood Preservers Institute. This is a 48-page engineering booklet that covers pole embedment and loading from a structural point of view. It is useful for builders with some engineering background who are designing pole buildings. It is available from the AWPI for $10.00.

The Solar Home Book, Bruce Anderson, Brick House Publishing Co., 34 Essex St., Andover, Massachusetts 01810. This is an excellent introduction to solar heating and cooling. This book was first published in 1976, but it is still one of the best solar primers on the market.

Wood-Frame House Construction, L.O. Anderson, U.S. Dept. of Agriculture, Agriculture Handbook No. 73, 1975. Available from the Superintendent of Documents, U.S. Government Printing Office, Washington, D.C. 20402. For a fraction of the price of a normal construction book, you can get this 220-page building book that covers all phases of house construction. It's a little dated, but still very useful and quite a bargain.

Wood Handbook: Wood As An Engineering Material, Forest Products Laboratory, Agriculture Handbook No. 72, U.S. Dept. of Agriculture. This is the best textbook available on the properties of wood, covering its strength, milling characteristics, strength of joints, preservation techniques, and other aspects of wood engineering. Available from the Superintendent of Documents, U.S. Government Printing Office, Washington, D.C. 20402.

Wood Structural Design Data, National Forest Products Association, 1978, 1619 Massachusetts Ave, N.W., Washington, D.C. 20036. This is a 248-page reference book listing safe loads for beams and joists given their size and span. It is available for $20.00 from the N.F.P.A. *Span Table For Joists and Rafters* is a simplified 44-page booklet that is available for $7.50. Write for their free list of technical publications.

Appendix B

Pole Suppliers
Members of the American Wood Preservers Institute

Arizona-Pacific Wood Preserving
PO Box 968
Eloy, Az. 85231

Atlantic Wood Industries, Inc.
PO Box 1608
Savannah, Ga. 31498

Augusta Wood Preserving Co.
PO Box 660
Orangeburg, S.C. 29115

B W Wood Products, Inc.
Rt. 1 PO Box 176
Manor, Ga. 31550

Baldwin Pole Piling Co.
PO Box 768
Bay Minette, Al. 36507

Barnes Lumber Corporation
PO Box 38
Charlottesville, Va. 22902

J. H. Baxter Co.
PO Box 5902
San Mateo, Ca. 94402

Bernuth Lumber Co., Inc.
201 Alhambra Circle
Coral Gables, Fl. 33134

Brown Wood Preserving Co.
PO Box 14234
Louisville, Ky. 40214

Central Wood Preserving, Inc.
PO Box 95
Slaughter, La. 70777

Coast Wood Preserving, Inc.
PO Box 673
Ukiah, Ca. 95482

Coastal Lumber Co.
PO Box 720
Marian, S.C. 29571

Coleman-Evans Wood Preserving
PO Box 1221
Jacksonville, Fl. 32201

Colfax Creosoting Co.
PO Box 231
Pineville, La. 71360

The Colwood Co., Inc.
PO Box 2688
Columbia, S.C. 29202

Conroe Creosoting Co.
PO Box 9
Conroe, Tx. 77301

Cook Lumber Co.
PO Box 17218
Orlando, Fl. 32860

Culpaper Wood Preservers
PO Box 260
Shelbyville, In. 46176

Dayton Flameproof Wood Co.
PO Box 38
Dayton, Oh. 45401

Elco Forest Products
PO Box 976
Opelousas, La. 70570

Escambia Treating Co.
PO Box 17108
Pensacola, Fl. 32522

Franwood Industries
PO Box 90
Farnwood, Ms. 39635

Fontana Wood Preserving
PO Box 1070
Fontana, Ca. 92335

General Timber, Inc.
PO Box 764
Sanford, N.C. 27330

Hart Creosoting Co.
PO Box 300
Jasper, Tx. 75951

Hatheway Patterson Co.
PO Box 177
Mansfield, Ma. 02048

Huxford Pole Timber Co.
PO Box 579
Huxford, Al. 36543

International Paper Co.
PO Box 809024
Dallas, Tx. 75380

Jennison-Wright Corp.
25550 Chagrin Blvd.
Cleveland, Oh. 44122

Koppers Co., Inc.
Kopper's Building
Pittsburg, Pa. 15219

Langdale Co.
PO Box 1088
Valdosts, Ga. 31630

Long Life Treated Wood, Inc.
PO Box 340
Hebron, Md. 21830

Lufkin Creosoting Co.
PO Box 1207
Lufkin, Tx. 75901

McCormick Baxter Creosoting Co.
300 Montgomery
San Francisco, Ca. 94104

McFarland Cascade
PO Box 1496
Tacoma, Wa. 98401

William C. Meredith Co.
PO Box 90456
East Point, Ga. 30364

National Wood Preservers, Inc.
PO Drawer F
Haverton, Pa. 19083

Neidermeyer-Martin Co.
1727 N.E. 11th Ave.
Portland, Or. 97212

Oliver-Celcure Wood Preservers
PO Box 29134
New Orleans, La. 70189

Pacific Wood Preservers of Bakerfield
5601 District Blvd.
Bakersfield, Ca. 93309

Permapost Products Co.
PO Box 100
Hillsboro, Or. 97123

Pressure Treated Timber Co.
3200 Gowen Rd.
Boise, Id. 83705

Rentokil, Inc.
PO Box 2249
Norcross, Ga. 30091

Ridge Lumber Industries
PO Box 1651
Lakeland, Fl. 33802

Shelby Wood Specialty, Inc.
PO Box 40
Selma, Ca. 93662

Southern Wood Piedmont Co.
PO Box 2006
Fernandina Beach, Fl. 32034

St. Regis Corporation
PO Box 26499
St. Louis Park, Mn. 55426

Stewart Lumber Company, Inc.
3359 Central Ave.
Minneapolis, Mn. 55418

John C. Taylor Lumber Sales, Inc.
PO Box 567
Beaverton, Or. 97005

Taylor-Ramsey Corp.
PO Box 11889
Lynchburg, Va. 24508

Tolleson Lumber Co., Inc.
PO Drawer E
Perry, Ga. 31069

Walker-Williams Lumber Co.
PO Box 170
Hatchachubbee, Al. 36858

Western Wood Preserving Corp.
PO Box L
Sumner, Wa. 98390

Wood Preservers Inc.
PO Box 1018
Warsaw, Va. 22572

Wyckoff Co.
1508 Peoples National Bank Bld.
Seattle, Wa. 98171

TECHNICAL ASSISTANCE

Mr. James S. Graham
National Timber Piling Council, Inc.
446 Park Ave.
Rye, N.Y. 10580

Mr. Kenneth E. Jurgens
Western Wood Preservers Institute
1499 Bayshore Highway #108
Burlingame, Ca. 94010

Manufacturers of Portable Sawmills

Portable Sawmills

Belsaw Machinery Co.
3679 Field Building
Kansas City, MO

Mighty Mite
International Enterprises of
    America, Inc.
PO Box 20066
Portland, OR   97220

Mobile Dimension Sawmill
Mobile Manufacturing Co.
Rt. 2 Box 22A
Sundial Road
Troutdale, OR   97218

Chain Saw Mills

Mark III Alaskan
Grandberg Industries, Inc.
200 S. Garrard Boulevard
Richmond, CA   94804

CLC Nordic Prince
CLC, Inc.
Box 189
LaGrande, OR   97850

George's 36″ Mill
George Prube
14135 Olde Hwy. 80
El Cajon, CA   92021

Sperber Chain Saw Mill
Sperber Tool Works, Inc.
Box 1224
West Caldwell, NJ   07006

Sun Angles

The following sun charts will help you plot the position of the sun at various times of the year for your particular latitude. You can use these sun charts to make sure your building site is not shaded by trees or other obstacles. You can also use them to calculate the necessary eave overhang that will shade windows in the summer but not block sunlight in the winter.

First, determine the latitude of your building site and select the sun chart that has the closest corresponding latitude. The *azimuth angle* refers to the position of the sun east or west of due south. True south is slightly different than magnetic south as determined with a compass. Consult a local topographical map to determine the *magnetic declination* of your area which will tell you how many degrees true south differs from magnetic south. The *altitude angle* refers to the height of the sun off the horizon.

The solid lines on the sun chart show the path of the sun during the day for different months of the year. The lowest line marks the sun's path on December 21, the shortest day of the year when the sun is lowest in the sky. The top line marks June 21, the longest day of the year, when the sun reaches it greatest altitude. The lines in between mark the sun's path during the two months that are equidistant from these solstices, such as May and July. The dotted lines are hour lines that mark where the sun is at any particular time of the day.

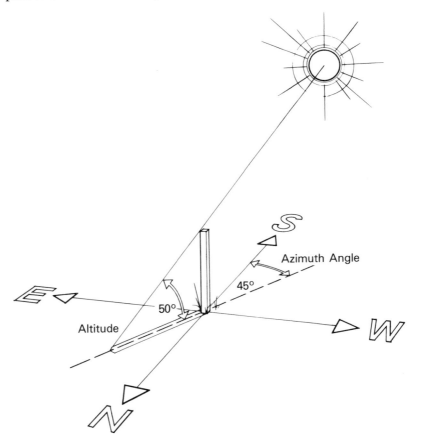

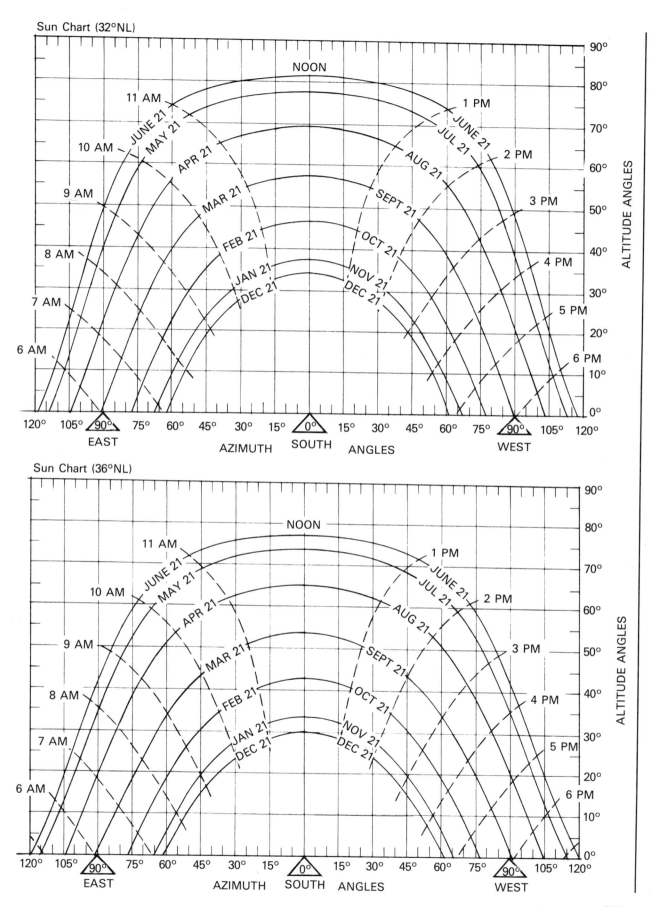

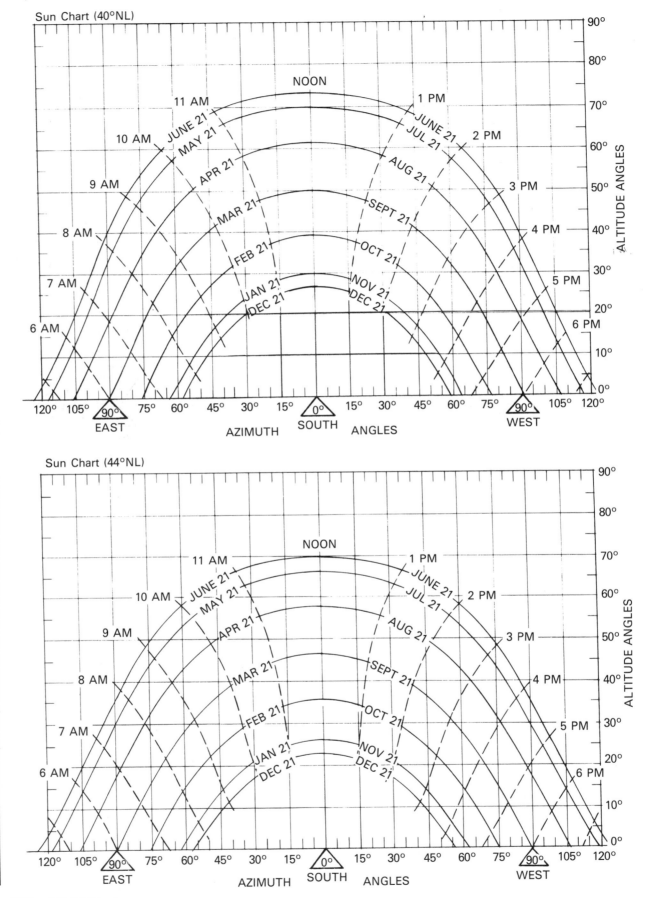

Sun Chart (40°NL)

Sun Chart (44°NL)

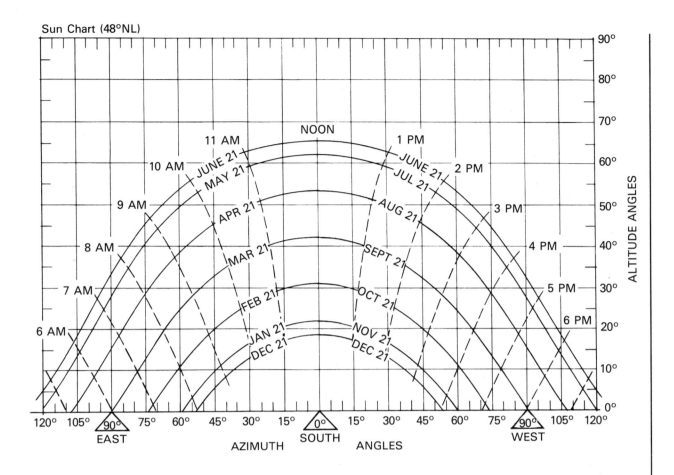

Sun Chart (48°NL)

Snow Loads

Snow Load In Pounds Per Square Foot
50 Year Mean Recurrence Interval

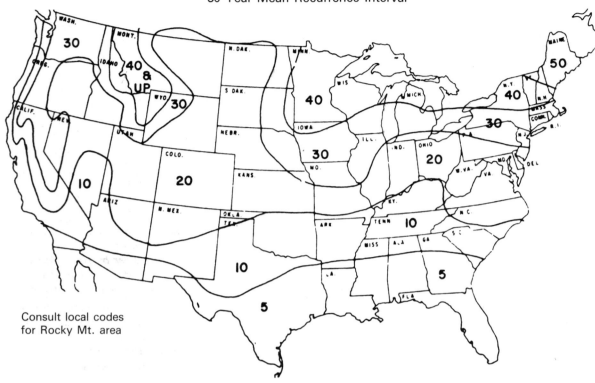

Consult local codes
for Rocky Mt. area

Adapted from: *Time Saver Standards for Architectural Design Data,* J. H. Callender,
McGraw Hill Book Co.

COMPARISON OF INSULATIONS USED IN RESIDENTIAL CONSTRUCTION

Material	R-value/inch	Available as	Appropriate applications	Specification
Cellulose	3.5	20-30 lb bags	• Wood framed • Ceilings, floors, walls	• Expect 10% settling • Good for retrofits • Specify by R-value rather than thickness
Fiberglass	3.14	20 lb bags	• Wood framed ceilings, floors • Walls	• Expect settling • Good for retrofits • Specify by R-value rather than thickness
Rockwool	2.9	20-30 lb bags	• Wood framed ceilings, floors • Walls	• Expect 10% settling • Good for retrofits • Specify by R-value rather than thickness
Perlite	2.7	20-30 lb bags	• Wood framed ceilings, floors	• Expect settling • Specify by R-value rather than thickness

Fibergalss or Mineral Wool	3.14	*Thicknesses:*
		  3-1/2, 6, 9, 12 inch
		Widths:
		  16, 24 inch
		• *Paper or foil faced*
			• *Wood framed ceilings, floors, walls*	• *Specify by thickness and width*
				• *Order by square footage*
				• *Install at full thickness*
				• *Requires fire protection*

Expanded Polystyrene (beadboard)	*3.6*	*Thicknesses:*
		  1, 2, 4 inch
		Surface Dimensions:
		  2×8
		  4×8
		• Squared edges
			• Interior insulative sheathing
			• Exterior insulative sheathing (above grade)
				• Requires protection from fire, UV degradation, and moisture
				• Use only compatible panel adhesives

Extruded Polystyrene (Blueboard or Pinkboard)
  smooth cell
  cut cell
	
	5.4
	4
		Thicknesses:
		  3/4, 1, 1-1/2, 2 inch
		Surface Dimensions:
		  2×8
		• T&G or squared edges
			• Interior insulative sheathing
			• Exterior insulative sheathing (above grade)
			• Interior foundation
			• Exterior foundation (below grade)
			• Beneath concrete slabs
			• Along slab edges
				• Requires protection from fire, UV degradation
				• Use only compatible panel adhesives and foundation sealants

Expanded Polyurethane	6.25	*Thicknesses:*
		  3/4, 1, 2, 4 inch
		Surface Dimensions:
		  4×8
		• Squared edges
		• Foil or wax paper facing
			• Interior insulative sheathing
			• Exterior insulative sheathing
				• Requires protection from fire

Polyisocyanurate	7.2	*Thicknesses:*
		  1, 1-1/4, 1-1/2, 1-3/4, 2, 2-1/4, 3 inch
		Surface Dimensions:
		  4×8
		• Squared edges
		• Foil or wax paper facing
			• Interior insulative sheathing
			• Exterior insulative sheathing
				• Requires protection from fire

Material	R-value/inch	Available as	Appropriate applications	Specification
Rigid Glass Fiberboard	4.4	*Thicknesses:* 1 inch *Surface Dimensions:* 4 × 8 4 × 9 • Squared edges • Foil facing	• Interior insulative sheathing	• Requires protection from fire

(From: Builders Guide to Solar Construction, R. Schlowsky, McGraw-Hill.)

Appendix G

HAY, BEDDING, AND FEED STORAGE SPACE REQUIREMENTS

Material	Weight Per Cubic Foot in Pounds	Cubic Feet Per Ton
Hay—Loose in shallow mows	4.0	512
Hay—Loose in deep mows	4.5	444
Hay—Baled loose	6	333
Hay—Baled tight	12	167
Hay—Chopped long cut	8	250
Hay—Chopped short cut	12	167
Straw—Loose	2-3	1000-667
Straw—Baled	4-6	500-333
Silage—Corn	35	57
Silage—Grass	40	50
Barley—48# 1 bu.	39	51
Corn, ear—70# 1 bu.	28	72
Corn, shelled—56# 1 bu.	45	44
Corn, cracked or corn meal—50# 1 bu.	40	50
Corn-and-cob meal—45# 1 bu.	36	56
Oats—32# 1 bu.	26	77
Oats, ground—22# 1 bu.	18	111
Oats, middlings—48# 1 bu.	39	51
Rye—56# 1 bu.	45	44
Wheat—60# 1 bu.	48	42
Soybeans—62# 1 bu.	50	40
Any small grain*	Use 4/5 of wt. of 1 bu.	
Most concentrates	45	44

(Courtesy: American Plywood Association.)

*To determine space required for any small grain use wheat (60# = 1 bu.) for example.
Then: 60 (4/5) = 48# wheat per cubic foot volume. To find number cubic feet wheat per ton, Then:

$$\frac{2000\# \text{ (Wt. of one ton)}}{48\# \text{ wheat per cubic foot volume}} = 42 \text{ cu. ft.}$$

TYPICAL MACHINERY DIMENSIONS

Machine	Feet	
	Length	Width
Tractors		
25–40 H.P.	12	6
40–70 H.P.	14	7
70–100 H.P.	15	8
4-wheel drive	16	10
Plows		
2 bottom	6	5
4 bottom	12	6
6 bottom	16	9
Tandem Disk		
7 ft.	10	7
10 ft.	11	10
14 ft.	12	14
Grain Drill		
12 × 7	7	8
23 × 6	9	16
Corn Planter		
4 row	12	14
6 row	12	20
Sprayer	10	7
Mower	8	8
Rake	13	11
Self-propelled Windrower		
7 ft. bar	10	10
12 ft. bar	11	17
16 ft. bar	12	20
Baler	17	13
Forage Harvester		
Extra Head	7	7
Blower	7	6
Combine		
Pulled, 8 ft.	21	11
Self-propelled, 14 ft.	24	16
Extra head, 4 row	7	12
Cotton Picker	20	11
Wagon	22	8
Manure Spreader	16	7
Manure Loader	14	6
Fertilizer Spreader	8	14
Pickup Truck	24	8

(From: Agricultural Buidlings and Structures, J. Whitaker, Reston Publishing, 1979.)

RECOMMENDED SCHEDULE FOR NAILING OF FRAMING AND SHEATHING

Joining	Nailing Method	Nails Number	Size	Placement
Header to joist	End-nail	3	16d	
Joist to sill or girder	Toenail	2	10d or	
		3	8d	
Header and stringer joist to sill	Toenail		10d	16 in. on center
Bridging to joist	Toenail each end	2	8d	
Ledger strip to beam, 2 in. thick		3	16d	At each joist
Subfloor, boards:				
1 by 6 in. and smaller		2	8d	To each joist
1 by 8 in.		3	8d	To each joist
Subfloor, plywood:				
At edges			8d	6 in. on center
At intermediate joists			8d	8 in. on center
Subfloor (2 by 6 in., T&G) to joist or girder	Blind-nail (casing) and face-nail	2	16d	
Soleplate to stud, horizontal assembly	End-nail	2	16d	At each stud
Top plate to stud	End-nail	2	16d	
Stud to soleplate	Toenail	4	8d	
Soleplate to joist or blocking	Face-nail		16d	16 in. on center
Doubled studs	Face-nail, stagger		10d	16 in. on center
End stud of intersecting wall to exterior wall stud	Face-nail		16d	16 in. on center
Upper top plate to lower top plate	Face-nail		16d	16 in. on center
Upper top plate, laps and intersections	Face-nail	2	16d	
Continuous header, two pieces, each edge			12d	12 in. on center
Ceiling joist to top wall plates	Toenail	3	8d	
Ceiling joist laps at partition	Face-nail	4	16d	
Rafter to top plate	Toe nail	2	8d	
Rafter to ceiling joist	Face-nail	5	10d	
Rafter to valley or hip rafter	Toenail	3	10d	
Ridge board to rafter	End-nail	3	10d	
Rafter to rafter through ridge board	Toenail	4	8d	
	Edge-nail	1	10d	
Collar beam to rafter:				
2 in. member	Face-nail	2	12d	
1 in. member	Face-nail	3	8d	
1-in. diagonal let-in brace to each stud and plate (4 nails at top)		2	8d	
Built-up corner studs:				
Studs to blocking	Face-nail	2	10d	Each side
Intersecting stud to corner studs	Face-nail		16d	12 in. on center
Built-up girders and beams, three or more members	Face-nail		20d	32 in. on center, each side
Wall sheathing:				
1 by 8 in. or less, horizontal	Face-nail	2	8d	At each stud
1 by 6 in. or greater, diagonal	Face-nail	3	8d	At each stud
Wall sheathing, vertically applied plywood:				
3/8 in. and less thick	Face-nail		6d	6 in. edge
1/2 in. and over thick	Face-nail		8d	12 in. intermediate

Joining	Nailing Method	Nails		
		Number	Size	Placement
Wall sheathing, vertically applied fiber-board:				
1/2 in. thick	Face-nail		1-1/2 in. roofing nail	3 in. edge and
25/32 in. thick	Face-nail		1-3/4 in. roofing nail	6 in. intermediate
Roof sheathing, boards, 4-, 6-, 8-in. width	Face-nail	2	8d	At each rafter
Roof sheathing, plywood:				
3/8 in. and less thick	Face-nail		6d	6 in. edge and 12 in. intermediate
1/2 in. and over thick	Face-nail		8d	

(From: Wood Frame House Construction, Agricultural Handbook No. 23, USDA.)

Index

More Good Books from

 **WILLIAMSON PUBLISHING**

BUILDING FENCES OF WOOD, STONE, METAL, & PLANTS
by John Vivian

Complete how-to on wood fence, stone fence, block, brick & mud fence, living fence & hedgerow, primitive fence, wire livestock fence, electric barrier fence, and classic horse fence.

192 pages, 8½×11, hundreds of drawings & photos, tables, charts.
Quality paperback, $13.95.

THE SHEEP RAISER'S MANUAL
by William Kruesi

"Don't raise sheep without it."—**The New Farm**

"Overall, The Sheep Raiser's Manual does a better job of integrating all aspects of sheep farming into a successful sheep enterprise than any other book published in the United States."—**Dr. Paul Saenger**
New England Farmer

280 pages, 6×9, illustrations, photos, charts & tables.
Quality paperback, $13.95.

KEEPING BEES
by John Vivian

Noted homesteader John Vivian packs his book with everything the beekeeper needs to know. Plenty of how-to including building your own hives, stands and feeders.

236 pages, 6×9, illustrations and step-by-step photos.
Quality paperback, $10.95.

SUMMER IN A JAR: Making Pickles, Jams & More
by Andrea Chesman

"With recipes this simple and varied, it's hard to find an excuse not to preserve summer in one's cupboard."—**Publishers Weekly**

Chesman introduces single jar recipes so you can make pickles and relishes a single quart at a time. Plenty of low-sugar jams, marmalades, relishes. Pickles by the crock, too. Outstanding recipes.

160 pages, 8¼×7¼, illustrations.
Quality paperback, $8.95.

GOLDE'S HOMEMADE COOKIES
by Golde Hoffman Soloway

"Cookies are her chosen realm and how sweet a world it is to visit."
—Publishers Weekly

Over 100 treasured recipes that defy description. Suffice it to say that no one could walk away from Golde's cookies without asking for another . . . plus the recipe.

144 pages, 8¼×7¼, illustrations.
Quality paperback, $8.95.

RAISING RABBITS SUCCESSFULLY
by Bob Bennett

"Here is one of the better books on raising rabbits."—**Booklist**

Written by one of the foremost rabbit authorities, this book is ideal for the beginning rabbit raiser, raising for food, fun, shows and profit.

192 pages, 6×9, illustrations and photos.
Quality paperback, $9.95.

RAISING POULTRY SUCCESSFULLY
by Will Graves

"An easy-to-understand beginner's guide to raising chickens, ducks, and geese. A good choice . . ."—**Library Journal**
Complete how-to for raising meat only, eggs only or a dual purpose flock. Warmly and expertly written.

196 pages, 6×9, illustrations, photos, tables.
Quality paperback, $9.95.

RAISING PIGS SUCCESSFULLY
by Kathy and Bob Kellogg

Everything you need to know for the perfect low-cost, low work pig raising operation. Choosing piglets, to housing, feeds, care, breeking, slaughtering, packaging, and even cooking your home grown pork.

224 pages, 6×9, illustrations, photos, tables.
Quality paperback, $9.95.

RAISING MILK GOATS SUCCESSFULLY
by Gail Luttmann

Complete coverage of everything involved in raising milk goats from selecting, feeds, housing, care, breeding, diagnosis by symptom, dairy goat business. Excellent.

192 pages, 6×9, photos.
Quality paperback, $9.95.

THE COMPLETE AND EASY GUIDE
TO SOCIAL SECURITY & MEDICARE
by Faustin F. Jehle

A lifesaver of a book for every senior citizen you know. Do someone a special favor, and give this book as a gift – written in "plain English" here's all that red tape unravelled.
"A goldmine of information about the most complicated system."
—Milicent Fenwick

175 pages, 8½×11½.
Quality paperback, $10.95.

HOME TANNING & LEATHERCRAFT SIMPLIFIED
by Kathy Kellog

"An exceptionally thorough and readable do-it-yourself book."
—Library Journal

192 pages, 6×9, step-by-step illustrations, photos, tanning recipes.
Quality paperback, $9.95.

DINING ON DECK: Fine Foods for Sailing & Boating
by Linda Vail

For Linda Vail a perfect day's sail includes fine food – quickly and easily prepared. She offers here 225 outstanding recipes (casual yet elegant food) with over 90 menus for everything from elegant weekends to hearty breakfasts and suppers for cool weather sailing. Her recipes are so good and so varied you'll use her cookbook year-round for sure!

160 pages, 8×10, illustrated.
Quality paperback, $10.95.

---

water damage to bottom corner & top of pages. 1-4-24 DC